CHILD LABOUR
IN
INDIAN SILK INDUSTRY

CHILD LABOUR IN INDIAN SILK INDUSTRY

DR. NIDHI SINHA

UPPAL PUBLISHING HOUSE
NEW DELHI—110 002

UPPAL PUBLISHING HOUSE
3, Ansari Road, Daryaganj, New Delhi-110002
Phones : *Off.* 3273756, 3286571 *Res.* 2242884

First Published 1994
ISBN. 81-85565-41-4

Printed in India

Published by B.S. Uppal for Uppal Publishing House
3, Ansari Road, Daryaganj, New Delhi-110002
and Printed at Sainion Printary, Delhi - 110032.

Preface

Child labour is prevalent in the developing countries as a consequence of their depleted national economy. India is no exception. The UNICEF has detected these areas and is doing its best to reduce children's suffering and brighten their future. But, somehow, child labour in the silk industry of Bhagalpur has escaped the notice of social researchers, so far. This dissertation, therefore, boldly projects the malaise pervading the silk industry of Bhagalpur, and einits backoning light to social workers, researchers, Parliamentarians, and Jurists to take up the issue of child labour on the social, politlcal and legal form to save poor children from deprivation and damage. This dissertation, coming out in the first decade of the International year of the child (IYC—1979), firmly establishes that the economics of Now" and "social justice of today" demand immediate care for the "poorest third of the mankind" for their individual development. Only then they can render vigrous social contribution tomorrow for human peace and prosperity.

To such an endeavour, thanks are due to Dr. Ziauddin Ahmed, M.A., Ph. D, presently Principal Patna College, and Dr. Moinuddin Raza, M.A., Ph.D., University Professor and Head of the Department of Sociology, Patna University, Patna, for their kind permission to work on the subject.

To my guide and my mother, Dr. Archana Sinha. M.A., D. Litt, University Professor and Head of the Department of Sociology, Magadh Mahila College, Patna, are offered my deepest regards for her continuous encouragement, enlightenment and occasional reproofs whenever I grew slack in this work which bring variety and richness to the topics discussed. My father, Dr. V.P. Sinha, M.Sc. Ph. D. filled me with a zeal to work and always gave me his helping hand.

My eldest Uncle, Dr. Surendra Prasad Sinha, M.A., Ph. D. Pro-Vice Chancellor, Mandar Vidyapith, is a colossus in the academic field. He loves to learn and to teach and his store of information is inexhaustible. He passed on his riches to me which are both the gold and glitter in the work.,

My father-in-law and mother-in-law, Sri Brahmdeo Prasad, Senior Advocate and Smt. Krishna Prasad were perennial source of inspiration for me, as also my elder brother-in-law, Sri Deepak Prasad, Personal Officer, Bharat Wagon & Engg. Co. Ltd. Likewise, my uncle and aunt, Dr. R.P. Okhandiar, M.B.B.S., FDS, Ph. D. and Mrs. Tara Okhandiar, extended all support to me to go ahead with the project. My cousin sister, Smt. Geeta Sinha and her son, Bablu, helped me to complete the Interview schedule. My elder sisters, Shubha and Ela, and their husbands Sri Amit Kumar, Dy. Superintending Engineer, ONGC, and Dr. Rajkumar Sinha, MBBS, M.D. deserve my respectful references in my work. My younger brother, Anshuman Sinha, rendered great assistance to me. Thanks to all of them, along with my grand mother and grand mother-in law.

To Dr. Santwana Das, M.A., Ph. D. Principal, Sharda Jhunjhunwala Mahila Mahavidyalaya, Bhagalpur and to Dr. Lalima Verma, M.A., Ph.D., B.Ed., L.L.B., Vice-Principal, my heartiest thanks for their cheers and co-operation.

But life's journey has been sweetened by the loving and profuse care and co-operation of my husband Sri Abhay Prasad, Advocate, and my little baby Ishita. His pat and her smile took away all the fatigue of laborious days and nights.

Sri Rajiv Ranjan Jha, M.A. is an adept in Statistical work. Thanks for his co-operation. For the help rendered to me by the Librarians of A.N. Sinha Institute of Social Sciences, Patna University Library, Central Library, Bhagalpur University, Bhagalpur and of National Library, Calcutta, I offer my gratitude.

Smt. Manju Bhattacharjee deserves commendation for a neat typing and for having helped me with a timely typescript.

Finally, to my respondents, the child labourers of Bhagalpur Silk industry, my heartfelt thanks for their co-operation, and I offer my prayers for their bright future which they richly deserve.

January, 1994 Dr. NIDHI SINHA
Patna—800 020

Contents

List of Tables

CHAPTER I

Introduction

Children have a claim on our conscience. For centuries we have promised them our love and care and caressed them so that they be impressed, but all along, we have never desisted from pledging their labour for a paltry sum. The watchful eyes of the Prophet of Proleteriat Revolution, Karl Marx, had keenly observed: "Now the capitalist system buys children and young persons under age. Previously, the workman sold his own labour-power, which he disposed of nominally as a free agent. Now he sells wife and child. He has become a slave-dealer".[1]

This may sound harsh, but is true beyond negation. What happened in Europe after the Industrial Revolution, happens today in the developing countries, including of course, the Latin America and the Carribean, on a very large scale. We have not been able to wipe out the difficult circumstances children live in, say in Africa, large part of Asia and Latin America. They lack the basic needs for existence: education and health, water and sanitation, food, security and nutrition and safety from infections and epidemics. All these can be

1. Marx, Karl, *Capital*, 1867.

obtained for the children at low societal and financial cost, but we are satisfied with preparing projects, leaving their implementation in the backyards.

For the mistakes of the adults, the children suffer. For the gory ambitions of the war-mongers, the children undergo penalties of hell. Let us turn our eyes to the street children in Latin America, suffering from AIDS, or children in war-ravaged Lebanon, Iran and Iraq, or Sudan, or in poverty-ridden Mozambique, Ethiopia, Angola, Botswana, Guinea, Mali, Mauritania, Senegal or in countries visited by natural calamities like, typhoom and earthquakes, as in Philippines, Indonesia, Malayasia, Bangladesh and Ecquador. Everywhere the same grim story seems to be repeating itself. Even the children of India, Pakistan and Afghanistan look askance, gazing into the vast ocean of blue vacuum. If they supplicate with a claim on the conscience of mature men, what wonder when there is no alternative ?

Naturally, the sad plight of the children has evoked great sympathy among educationists, philanthropists, social and political thinkers. Some by simple statements, holding out big promises, and some by pinching banters have aroused our senses to the unredeemed task towards the flower of human society. The great pen-man Horace Mann emphatically wrote : "Republic, one after another....have perished from a want of intelligence and virtue in the masses of the people....If we do not prepare children to become good citizens, if we do not enrich their minds with knowledge, imbue their hearts with love of truth and duty, and a reverence for all things sacred and holy, then our republic must go down to destruction, as others have gone before it; and mankind must sweep through another vast cycle of sin and suffering, before the dawn of a better era can arise upon the world."[2]

2. Mann, Horace—In New York Times, Sept., 15, 1953.

The great pioneer of child education, Maria Montessori, rightly hinted: "Humanity shows itself in all its intellectual splendour during this tendor age as the sun shows itself at the dawn, and the flower in its first unfolding of the petals; and we must respect religiously, reverently, these first indications of individuality. If any educational act is to be officacious, it will be only that which tends to help toward the complete unfolding of this life. To be thus helpful it is necessary rigorously to avoid the arrest of spontanecous movements and the imposition of arbitrary tasks. It is, of course, understood that here we do not speak of useless or dangerous acts, for these must be suppressed, destroyd...".

To understand the necessity and immediacy of such educational projects we must turn to an approach that is antithetic but is an eye-opener. Speaking about the German child's training during the Nazi regime, Robert Ley in his Army Talks on April 24, 1945, gave out in detail: "We begin with the child of three. As soon as he begins to think, we press a little flag into his hand. Then comes school, Hitler Youth, the Storm Troops, military service. We do not leave him alone for one minute. When all that is over, the Labour Front comes and takes possession of him again, and does not let him go until death." The consequence of such steel framed-education is the grimmest tragedy of the twentieth century German history. Long ago, in 1851, Arthur Schopenhauer had warned that "no child under the age of fifteen should receive instruction in subjects which may possibly be the vehicle of serious error, such as philosophy or religion, for wrong notions imbibed early can seldom be rooted out, and of all the intellectual faculties, judgement is the last to arrive at maturity." Nazis never cared for the Vedantist Schopenhauer, but they cared for Niotcsche whose philosophy of nihilism brought Germany to ruins. Fundamentalism, in whatever garb it comes, is opposed to humanism, and is the greatest enemy of human progress of world peace. Examples are not difficult to find. Entire Asia is witnessing religion or political fundamentalism, as a result of which, annihilation of life in general may take place here and hopes of global peace evaporate.

Child mind must blossom like a garden-fiower taking all its virtues from nature. He will be a full man if he learns the values of love and reciprocity. His surroundings are his greatest teachers. They learn by imitation both kindliness and cruelty, and the adults, father, mother, friend, set for them the examples of conduct. John Ruskin rightly mentioned that to make your children capable of honesty is the beginning of education. But the best advice comes from Josiah Warren who wrote in 1855: "To solve the problem of education children must be surrounded with equity and must be equitably treated, and each and everyone, parent or child, must be understood to be an individual, and must have his or her individual rights equitably respected."[3]

But, for the proverb: Easier said than done. Individual rights and child labour do not go together ethically. Denial of individual rights to children is best referred to in a poem of banter:

> "The golf links lie so near the mill
> That almost any day
> The labouring children can look out
> And see the men at play.[4]

Therefore, to round up the whole tale, a word of advice from Isadora Duncan is serene and quite apt :

"So long as little children are allowed to suffer, there is no true love in this world.[5]

3. Taken from the Great Quotations, compiled by Seldes, George. Pocket Book Series, New York, p. 145.
4. Ibid., Saruh N. Cleghorn, p. 143.
5. Ibid., p. 143, spoken in 1924 at Berlin.

In the modern world totalitarianism tramples over the seeds of socialism and that is, and was, the perennial cause of revolutions, insurrections, and terrorisms. John Adams had spoken an eternal truth when he said : "In every society where property exists there will ever be a struggle between rich and poor. Mixed in one assembly, equal laws can never be expected; they will either be made by the members to plunder the few who are rich, or by the influence to fleece the many who are poor." This was like anticipating Karl Marx who later bluntly said, "The rich will do everything for the poor but get off their backs." Not that the poor have no guilt in the affair. They administer to the idleness of the rich by their subjugation and therefore, the rich in return find the best methods of confirming the slavery and increasing the burdens of the poor. The result is that millions toil but the fruits go to a few who are rich and who hold the strings of both the private and governmental purse. In his famous book, *Un to The Last*, which left indelible impression on Mahatma Gandhi, John Ruskin had boldly asserted : "whereas it has been known and declared that the poor have no right to the property of the rich, I wish it also to be known and declared that the rich have no right to the property of the poor." Gandhiji went much farther. He advocated Trusteeship of the poor by the rich. But this has remained a wishful thinking even half a century after his martyrdom. Instead, the bitter truth spoken by Plato, the Immortal thinker, stands vindicated even today. He had advised people to realise for their own good : "Any ordinary city is in fact two cities, one the city of the poor, the other of the rich, each at war with the other; and in either division there are smallest ones—you would make a great mistake if you treated them as single states."[6] Bhagalpur city with a population of about 3 lakhs has the two compartments and is no exception as long as child labour in silk industry exists. It carries with itself all the

6. Plato, *The Republic*, b. 7. Section 423 (Tr. by Jowett).

symptoms of neglect of the child labour, as if time has stopped moving on its wheels for the working kids, and they live in the age-old dark chambar of illiteracy, ill-health, insufficiency and insignificance which are the attributes of poverty and pauperism.

No country's will is determined by itself alone. We interdepend, even though some are affluent and some are not. This is yet another dimension to the the problem of poverty whose offshoot is child labour. No live in an era of common market, world trade, loans, aids, International Monetary Fund, favourable and adverse trade balances, debts, repayments, rising and falling prices of commodity and human labour, a search for a Grand Alliance between nations and communities, between government and private organizations, who are in search for peace and prosperity. We jointly search for ways and means to monitor and evaluate programme for social mobilization, and awareness of legal energies are on the anvil, and all the powers, great and small, are seeking to raise their economic standard. Even then rising debts and falling incomes are a phenomenon easily discernible in the developing countries. This breeds poverty. Let us catch the real picture :

"Two elements have dominated the deterioration of economic prospects over so much of the developing world in recent years. They are rising debt repayment and falling commodity prices.

"The total debt of the developing world is now over U.S. $ 1000 billion. In many countries, annual repayments of interest and capital amount to more than the total of all new aids and loans being received each year. On average, repayments now claim almost 25% of the developing world's export revenues.

"Meanwhile, as outgoings have risen, income has declined. The developing world still depends on raw materials for the majority of its export earnings. But in the last ten years, real prices for the developing world's provincial commodities—including fuels, minerals, jute, rubber, coffee, cocoa, tea, oils, fats, tobacco, and timber—have fallen by approximately thirty percent."[7]

There is no illusion greater than the belief that money flows from rich nations to the poor nations to assist in the struggle against poverty. Instead the flow is from the poor countries to the richer ones in the shape of payment of loans, aids, interests repayments and return of capital. The annual flow from the poor to the rich is estimated at $ 60 billion each year.

As such, "for much of the developing world, the economic climate has therefore darkened quite dramatically in the last decade. As a result, most of the affected nations have been forced to adopt economic adjustment policies in an attempt to stave off balance of payments crises, while at the same time meeting debt obligations, maintainning essential imports and struggling to return to economic growth."[8] Over 70 developing nations are struggling to adjust their economies by adopting methods of dampening down public demands, devaluation of currency, a withdrawal of subsidies on fuel and staple food-stuffs and deep cuts in governmant spending. Naturally, the poor suffer more and more, which includes their children also. This suffering is caused by two factors which the eminent writer puts as follows :

"The first is that the poor have the least 'economic fat' with which to absorb the flow of recession. Often, three quarters of the income of the very poor is spent on food and much of what remains is needed for fuel and water, housing and clothes, bus fares and medical treatment" . . . .

"The second reason is that the poor also have the least 'political muscle' to ward off that blow. Services which are of

7. *The State of the World's Children, 1989*, published by UNICEF, p. 15.
8. Ibid.

concern to the richer and more powerful sections of society such as the major hospitals, universities, the national airlines, prestige development projects, and the military—have not borne a proportionate share of the cuts in publice spending. With some honourable exceptions, the services which have been most radically pruned are health services, free primary education, and food and fuel subsidies—the services on which the poor are most dependent and which they have least opportunity to replace by any other private means."[9]

India is one such among the developing countries that is bogged down in debt trap. "The deficits in trade balances keep on increasing annually despite attempts at export promotion and import substitution."[10] The picture is still gloomy. We are being churned between fresh borrowings and old repayments. It is like a poor family dependent on borrowings and more borrowings to pay off back loans. Sometimes after, even friends and well wishers will tighten their purse strings and leave us to loan-sharks or to rot in bankruptcy. India's adverse trade balance is well high 10,000 crores, as a consequence of which developmental programmes at the grass roots are more honoured in their breach than in application. As a natural corollary, children are being pressed into service to augment family income because family subsistence has become an insurmountable problem when prices are soaring upward and daily income is falling downward. This spectacle is true of children employed in the silk industry of Bhagalpur, as this is true elsewhere also where children are employed to improve family income.

Here comes UNICEF (a branch of UNO) to give succour to

9. Ibid., p. 16.
10. The Times Magazine—*Economy*—New Delhi, 1988, p. 113. "Our export rose steeply to Rs. 15,719 crores and were less than our imports (Rs. 22,343 crores) by only Rs. 6,624 crores (in the year 1987-88). The government, for some years, has been repaying carlier loans through fresh borrowings"....

the children all over the world who suffer incredibly due to rich man's lust and irrational national economic policy. The UNICEF come as a saviour of children who look at all their problems in a wide sweep. The UNICEF, short form of "United Nations International Children's Emergency Fund" was created by a unanimous decision of United Nations General Assembly on 11 December, 1946 with the mandate to help protect the lives of children and promote their development. Poverty and destitute children are the legacies of world wars, but kindly gentlemen would not let them go to dogs. They would do their utmost to redeem the victims of war and enable them to begin their lives with a fresh zeal, and an in-born hope. The need to resuscitate the child came to the United Nations Organizations spontaneously. A Declaration of the Rights of the child (also called the Declaration of Geneva) was unanimously passed on the 20th November, 1959. The declaration recognised that mankind owns to the child the best that it has to give, and therefore resolved :

1. The child must be protected beyond and above all considerations of race, nationality or creed.
2. The child must be cared for with due respect for the family as an entity.
3. The child must be given the means requisite for its normal development, materially, morally, and spiritually.
4. The child that is hungry must be fed ; the child that is sick must be nursed ; the child that is physically or mentally handicapped must be helped ; the maladjusted child must be reeducated ; the orphan and the waif must be sheltered and succoured.
5. The child must be the first to receive relief in times of distress ;
6. The child must enjoy the full benefits provided by social

welfare and social security schemes ; the child must receive a training which will enable it, at the right time, to earn a livelihood, and must be protected against every form of exploitation.

7. The child must be brought up in the consciousness that its talents must be devoted to the service of its fellowmen.

These declarations form the guiding principles for several national and international agencies[11] working for the uplift of the child. More than that all the legislations enacted mitigating the rigours of child labaur, draw their inspirations from these noble declarations. From 1959 onwards the "UNICEF not only seeks government and public support for programmes of co-operation but also tries to stimulate public awareness of children's needs and the means to meet them by advocacy—with governments, civic leaders, educators and other profes sional and cultural groups, the media and local communities. For this reason, UNICEF greatly values its partnership with National Committees for UNICEF and its working relationship with nongovernmental organizations for industrialized as well as developing countries."[12] It was at the instance of the UNICEF that 1979 was declared the International Year of the Child (IYC) on the 20th anniversary of the Declaration of the Rights of the Child. In consequence thereof much light has been thrown on the conditions of children, labouring and living silently in the throes of death. The IYC helped to spot out areas where children's conditions were unimaginably bad and was moving towards something worse. It raised a cry for

11. These may be enumerated as (1) Union Department of Rural Development, (2) Union Department of Social Welfare, (3) Union Department of Health, (4) Union Deportment of Food, (5) Central Social Welfare Board, (6) Meals for the Millions, (7) CARE, (8) National Christian Council, (9) UNICEF, (10) FAO, (11) W.H.O.

12. A brochure entitled : What UNICFF is and Does, 1989.

reducing inequality in whatever form it existed and also for establishing social justice. All the media went up the air to ventilate the sad plight of children and the utter necessity to save precious lives all over the globe, without any delay. A rich crop of literature also grew up to impress readers and even journals did not lag behind. All of them helped people to understand the severity and the magnitude of the problem, especially of the working child, the diminishing child and our social commitment towards the child in distress. The labouring child gave out one thing in common—that they are a mercilessly exploited community.

This brings us to our main problem of study: "Child Labour in the Silk Industry of Bhaglapur—A Sociological Study" Scientific study rests on analytic outlook or part by part studies in order to comprehend the whole. What may apply to the child labour in the silk industry of Bhagalpur may also relate itself to the child labour engaged in other spheres of production. The child at the loom in Bhagalpur is as much a pitiable sight as the child with sulphur and phosphorus in Sivakasi or with jute dust at Bhadohi in Uttar Pradesh. An empirical study therefore, depends on four elements, viz,

(1) Perception, which means awareness of a problem or situation,

(2) Motivation, meaning thereby a desire or a feeling to see improvements in the situation,

(3) Knowledge and skill-which are the instrument to effect reforms, and

(4) The means to act, which includes the will, the fund to monitor necessary mutations and the legal backing so that society may be urged to adopt essential changes.

The researcher has fully realized the value of children in the present and the future times. She has also comprehended child labour in its beneficial and ugly aspects and she has also felt the necessity of ameliorating their conditions through legal measures, through harnessing modern mass communication techniques as a social marketing strategy of national rules and laws. This will go a long way to strengthen the UNICEF mass growth movement for child welfare and people's enlightenment as regards our pious commitment to every child in the world. For this purpose the dissertation has been divided into six Chapters apart from introduction and conclusion and a rich bibliography embracing all the essential factors for study. Chapter One looks into the values of child religiously, socially-universally, and while referring to the absence of child labour system in ancient scriptures, discovers its prevalence with feudalism, then industrialized society, growth of monopoly in trade and the craze for unlimited powers which can come only through killing social norms in public and poltical life. The chapter then switches on to silk industry which is very much ancient; it is mentioned in the Rigvedic mantras. Chinese silk is as old as history, from whom Greeks have inherited knowledge in silk manufacture. Europe got it via Constantinople, and the knowledge spread to Africa, Spain, Portugal and Sicily. In India silk manufacture has an unbroken history. While there are numerous references to silk is Hindu epics and subsequent literatures, the Mughals too kept up their fascination for silk intact. Trading in silk was brisk during the East India Company rule in India and Cassimbazar, Hugli, Patna, Agra and Bhagalpur were silk trading centres of eminence, dealing especially in Eri, Mulbery, Tasar and Monga qualities. Maldah prepared silk and cotton mixed fabric which is called Bafta. Rearing Cocoons is Tribal's agro-economic base for their livelihood, in which Rajmahal district excelled.

In Post-Independent India, silk trade is being patronised. In Bhagalpur Division six demonstration centres, viz. at Sabour, Pirpainti, Birpur, Naugachia, Gopalpur, and Akbarnagar have been opened. Champanagar, Nathnagar and Akbarnagar which comprise silk manufacturing centres in

Bhagalpur city take in child as labourers which they earn and learn about processes of preparing silk cloth.

Child labour is defined in Chapter Two as a social problem since it hinders, arrests or distorts the natural growth of children is an atmosphere of servility. It is different from voluntary efforts at learning a trade or a Basic manual training in schools or Ashramas for self-help scheme. This Chapter also deals with causes of the prevalence of child labour, the cardinal ones being illiteracy, extreme poverty, enticement by employers, absence of trade union, runaways or castaways from homes, a bit of adventurism, or pledging by parents or guardians and such others.

This Chapter also portrays a statewise picture of child engaged in diverse jobs. Andhra Pradesh leading, Bihar, Madhya Pradesh, West Bengal trailing, and Kerala at the rear end. Areas of children's employments are also illumined in the Chapter. Of course, child labour in rural front is not taken to account, so also begging but the difference between urban and rural job opportunities are clearly brought out. Yet what is wanting in published report is a mention of child labour engaged in the silk industry of Bhagalpur. This is the real contribution of the researcher at work in this dissertation that she has been able to bring the issue into limelight alongwith the varieties of jobs, light and heavy, manual and mechanical, solid and chemical. As such, this chapter gives a four-dimensional picture of child labour in silk industry of Bhagalpur which is further clarified with the help of questionnaire schedule, appended at the end of the work.

Chapter Three reviews literature on child and child labour. There has been a great paucity of informative literature on the subject until recently. Dickens in English literature and Mark Twain in the American were the first writers drawing people's attention to the painful existence of children working in chimneys or working as Negro slaves. India, of course, lacked such enlightening works in prose or poetry.

But real investigative literature on child labour began in England in 1908 by A.J. Beveridge which was followed by an important work entitled "The International Hand Book of Child Care and Protection" by F. Fuller in 1928. Lumpkin brought out his first book on child labour in America in 1937. Bolshevik Russia did not have child labour problem. The United States of America opened a Children Bureau' under the Department of Labour which took care of these hostages of fortune.

World War I left millions of children as orphans and their upbringing caused real headache to politicians and social workers. World War II came too soon and the disaster was unimaginably great, especially in regards to children. World attention was at once drawn to these war orphans and destitutes. However, with the establishment of the United Nations Organization and its numerous agencies, UNESCO, UNICEF FAO, W.H.O., I.L.O., and others great concern was expressed for children, valuable global studies were made, ways and means to improve their lot were discovered and utilised and finally legal measures against child labour were brought into force.

Naturally, a rich crop of literature was produced year after year as peace dawned on earth. U.N.O.'s sacred resolution to avoid war in all cases acted as a balm on the bruised souls of war victims when human rights and fundamental freedom were firmly established. UNICEF and W.H.O. took care of the world children as never before. India too followed suit with the help of National Children Board and Indian Council for Child Welfare (ICCW). Bihar took a cue from these efforts. An Annual Report in the working of the Employment of Children Act 1938, prepared by the Labour Department (Factories), Government of Bihar (Ranchi), was published in 1965. The International Labour Organization suggested more and more protective measures for working children in which jurists, legislators and social workers joined hands. All these agencies brought out numerous literatures on child labour, and for mitigating their lot, they advocated full co-operation of the private social agencies and voluntary organizations with the governmental measures. They plainly said child reform is social reform and the name of the child is TODAY. Mrs. Tara Ali Baig's efforts in this direction are stupendous. She had a holistic approach—a child is a being pulsating with desires and ambitions and given an opportunity he will prove his worth. As such a child must be cared for on his physical, mental, moral or spiritual front. Her works are of immense value.

The declaration of 1979 as the International Year of the Child (IYC) just twenty years after the declaration of the Rights of Child (1959) gave a fillip to many writers to produce books of great merit. Books by D. Paul Choudhary, member of the Social Welfare Board, Alfred de Souza, Alakh Narayan Sharma, Leela Gulati and many others have produced either a compendium of essential services for help to children, or have given us regional studies, e.g. of Kerala, Bihar, Tamil Nadu, Uttar Pradesh, Gujarat and other parts.

The Five Year Plans have further offered incentives to prepare illuminating literatures on child labour, as well as, they record remedial beneficial measures covering children's interest. The contribution of journals and newspapers are not small, instead they have vividly brought to public view the outrageous conditions in which child labour exists in India. They are the real sentinels of India's democracy. The din caused by newspaper has compelled private agencies, voluntary organisations to join issue with governmental efforts to improve conditions of labouring children. For example, The Times of India, March 27, 1988, issued from Patna, pointed out that Bhagalpur manufactures 50 to 80 lakh metres of Tessar which is exported to Germany, France, U.S.A., Japan, U.K., Italy, Switzerland, and Spain. Bihar produces 70 to 80 percent of

India's silk which is varied and cheaper than other's products. In essence, silk manufacture of Bhagalpur is a vital small scale industrial output of great magnitude helping to reduce foreign adverse trade balances, yet the fate of the child labour in Bhagalpur silk industry remains what it was fifty years back.

Yet these literatures arouse a feeling of urgency among social workers to awaken social conscience and a motivation to render our best services to the labouring children. When perception and motivation join hands, the ways open by themselves for immediate reform.

Our plans and proposals and the sphere of study are given in Chapter Four called Methodology. In recent times empirical study is more favoured than mere descriptive study because the former is impersonal, objective, logical, scientific and suitable for checks and analysis. Any social study relates itself to interaction of human relations and aims at finding solutions and decisions.

Hypothesis shows us the problem, as in the present case it is about child labour in the silk industry of Bhagalpur. The necessity for such a study arose from a severe lacking of information on the subject.

Sociological hypothesis is studied in a setting, a background of men and their surrounding. The men about whom such a study is to be carried through make the sample, of course, to be more rational, a part of the whole people is sampled out for research and study. What is true about a part, or a stratum, is quite logically true for the entire strata, as a grain of cooked rice speaks for the entire rice in the cooking pot. In the present cases, the entire area of Bhagalpur Municipal Corporation is the universe, the weaver's workhouse comprise the setting and the working children (the respondents) and their parents make the sample. Nearly 250 cases of respondents have been taken up for sample study.

Modernization and urbanization are overtaking Bhagalpur rapidly. The place has all the modern amenities—university, Rail-Road connections, Post and Telegraph, and has Science Colleges, Medical, Engineering and Agricultural Colleges, apart from numerous Arts and Commerce teaching institutions. The population is mixed in respect of caste, creed, language, and other items. We have therefore sought to study the hypothesis under such variables as socio-economic factors, age-group, educational level, occupational structure, Income category, types of family, castes and religions. Our respondents are 122 from rural area comprising 48.80% of the samples and 128 persons from urban area making 51.20%. Among the child labour, illiterates and boys-girls upto Primary standard make a big chunk and their parents mostly belong to agriculture or manual labour profession. The largest number of respondents fall in the income group of Rs. 5,000/- to Rs. 10,000/- annually. Their families are mostly small and nuclear: Scheduled castes respondents abound the scene and Muslim Julahas or Momins are considerable.

We have gained these figures through data collection made by Interview schedule which comprise of personal informations about the respondents and also about employer-employee relationship, as well as legal awareness about child protection laws. The whole process is investigative and objective in spirit.

Chapter Five deals with interpretation of data collected through Interview schedule. These data give us a glimpse of the life of the child labourer engaged in Bhagalpur silk industry. It is like a mirror that clearly reflects the social life, labouring children's (and sometimes their parent's also) opinions, aspirations, perception, motivation in the background of the jobs they perform. The jobs have been divided into three categories, viz., Primary, Secondary and the Final work. Ample numbers of illustrative Tables have been offered which inform us statistically on vital questions. In the primary work children from 5-7 years of age do Nari and Bai filling work, but they sit for long hours which subsequently cripples their backbones. Children between 11 to 15 years sit at the spinning wheel all day long thereby paying a heavy price in the form of physical deformity. Questions have been asked regarding sanitation of the surrounding, availability of light and drinking water, no toilet amenities, as a result of which about 86.40% of child labour undergo a physical process of slow diminishing. Electric fans cannot be dreamed of even though Bhagalpur summer temperature ranges from 35° to 42° celsius.

Questions regarding hours of work, leisure, weekly off days and holidays in a month have been asked which elicited valuable informations. Leisure may be enjoyed for a period of 30 to 60 minutes during a working period of 8 to 12 hours a day. Wages form an important subject of query, as such amount of wages, mode of payment, security deposits, cut in payment of wages due, are valid questions have been put to the respondents. Method of utilising leisure and also utility of wages (whether on himself, or in family, or deposits as savings) are further interrogations through the Interview schedule. Whether wages earned are satisfactory or not is also a pertinent point which has been raised before the respondents. One thing that arose in common was that labour and wages are not commensurate with each other. In other words, they are very low. Only 24.40% pleaded satisfaction. 73.60% expressed dissatisfaction. Education, age-group and Income status are all along the main variables in dealing with the respondents. Their opinion about job-satisfaction was also valuable. 74.80% expressed distress with their jobs which were monotonous, and had no promotional avenues. 1.60% had nothing to say, whereas 23.60% felt satisfied with their lot. The respondents also expressed much in favour of job insecurity. 62.40% expressed themselves insecure as they were casual or temporary labour.

Towards the end, some statements were put before the respondents and were asked to indicate their agreement or otherwise. On being asked if they (the child labourers) were given greater attention in their homes, 87.60% said yes. To the second statement that jobs gave them self confidence 52.40% said yes, and to the third statement whether such an employment brought them economic independence, only 17.20% agreed telling that they live in a family and the family and they are interdependent as such the question of economic independence does not arise.

Finally, the last item to be treated in the Interview Schedule was about legal awareness among parents. Only 8.40% (father) and 0.40% (mother) know about children employment and protective laws from Trade Unions, Radio and Television. Others had no knowledge of legal enactments regulating employer-employee relationship as regards child labour. Lack of Legislative awareness is helping the perpetuation of the social evil, that is, employing child labour for profiteering and selfishness.

Naturally, we come to Chapter Six which treats the subject of legal measures and people's awareness of the same as regards employment of children in any industry. Since social laws have certain roots in the history of a nation, we have briefly indicated that ancient Indian policy did not approve of employment of children. According to Kautilya, child labour was prevalent among the Greeks, yet in India too, pledging of child or any member of the family and his restitution was possible on payment of debts. Arya and Dasa were contradictory terms even according to Manu. During Mughal time certain crafts like weaving, stone polishing or cutting diamonds or even filigree works were patronised. The Britishers deeply appreciated muslins, silk and other Indian handicrafts and whatsoever their opposition to local cloth manufacturers, they are the pioneers of making labour laws, more particularly, protective laws for labouring children. We may safely divide the British period under three sub-periods, viz, the middle of the 19th century (1850 onwards) as the period of initiating children's employment laws, the second phase from 1921-1930 as the time for substantial progress, and from 1931-1947 as period of documentation and comprehensive reports. Anyway the post-independent era from 1947 to date is full of progressive efforts, of constant discussions and implementation of legislative efforts. The avenue is still open for more improvements in framing protective laws for working children.

Apprentices Act was passed in 1850, Guardianship and Wards Act was passed in 1890 which is in fact the precursor to Adoption Act of 1979. Factories Act was passed in 1881 and eight such Acts were passed between 1881 and 1961.

The close of the Second World War brought into existence the UNO under whose aegis grew many agencies looking into children's problems. The UNICEF stole the show for the child and became its paramount spokesman. They have suggested an International Summit to discuss comprehensively the situations that surround the child all over the globe. Even SAARC countries have endorsed this view and consider it an urgent task especially for the developing countries.

The human aspect regarding labouring child is first noticed in the Factories Act of 1881, which was the first to lay down that a child below 7 years will not work, a child above 7 years will not work in two establishments any day, working hours shall be 9 hours from morning to evening and a child will be given four holidays in a month. Obviously, some of the clauses deserved reconsideration and they were amended in 1891. Age of the working child was raised to 9 years, working hours were reduced to 7 hours. In 1901 it was further amended as working hours only 6, Age certificate and certificate of fitness were made essential and all dangerous machine would be fenced. Better times came in 1922 with the advent of International Labour Convention. Age raised to 15 years, only six hours work, half an hour's rest for meal and by 1933, a machinery of Inspector was established to keep watch on the working of the factories where 20 men were employed. In 1937 came the children's pledging of Labour Act and children up to 13 years would not be put as working hands in Transport of goods, passengers, at wharves, docks, quays etc. Soon after, in 1938, came the Employment of Children Act which imposed certain duties on the employers and certain amenities for child-labour. Thereafter a spate of reforms in law took place in 1940, 1941, 1944, 1945, 1946 and 1947.

After Independence, the Constitution of Ihdia guaranteed rights of free development of a child both in its Fundamental Riehts and Directive Principles. Later legislations are based on the liberal spirit of Fundamental Rights and Directive Principles. Consequently, The Children Act of 1960, amended up to 1981 define echildren, their hours of work, children's homes, rules for neglected and delinquents. The Act demands the employers of child ladour to maintain their register and display essential clauses of the Act for the information of the children at work.

Yet, there is a gap, a serious one for that matter. Bhagalpur silk industry does not offer any proof of maintaining what this Act of 1960, amended up to 1981, demands from them. Nobody has paid attention to this lapse, although there exists the National Children's Board with Prime Minister as its President and eminent ministers as its members.

But the worst part of the story is the complete absence of people's awareness of the enactments made to save children from exploitation. Only one mother and about half a dozen father could say that they had heard of legal measures. Lack of social awareness beats the purpose of legislative measures. If Bhagalpur silk industry is in danger from an invasion by nylon and synthetic yarn fabrics, the child labour in Bhagalpur silk industry is in the continuous risk of severe exploitation because of his ignorance of the rights offered to him in the Constitution's Fundamental Rights and those inscribed in the

Directive Principles. Voluntary organizations, social workers, Jurists and philanthropists have to come forward to propagate these redeeming measures, just as they are required to preach from house tops the safeties granted to women in Anti-Dowry legislation. Both the Children Act and the Anti-Dowry Acts suffer for want of public information. The laudable efforts of UNICEF and allied agencies can succeed only when awareness of rights and duties are brought to the doors of people.

Thus this dissertation seeks to disseminate knowledge about child labour in Bhagalpur silk indusry, an unexplored area, an area off the bounds of sociological study so far, and in consequence it may spark off more investigative and empirical study, for which purpose the present work is entitled to be called a pioneer effort. Human rights are constricted due to inadequacy of information, called ignorance. William Hazlitt, the great thinker and writer was prudent enough to remark : "If mankind had wished for what is right, they might have had it long ago."

CHAPTER II

Silk from Ancient to Modern Times

A child is the crowning glory of a happy home. A well bred child is like a well cut diamond spreading its lustre and joy, wherever it is treasured. Rightly did William Wordsworth say :

"Thou liest in Abraham's bosom all the year,
And worshipp'st at the Temple's inner shrine,
God being with thee when we know it not."[1]

A child is both ignorant and innocent. Ignorance is his bliss as he does not know 'what Man has made of Man'. And innocence is his magical charm that gives his gestures pleasant grace.[2] Divinity and lamb-like meekness and closeness to the Heavenly Father are the great gift of a child, born either in a destitute or an affluent family. His innocence has to be pre-

I. Wordsworth, William, "By the Sea".

2. The Holly Bible—St. Matthews—18:3-5. "Except ye be converted and become as little children, Ye shall not enter into the Kingdom of heaven". "Whosoever therefore shall humble himself as this little child, the same is greatest in the Kingdom of heaven". "And who so shall receive one such little child in my name receiveth me."

served even while his ignorance has to be reduced in stages, by parents, society, and the state. To turn to Wordworth again—We have a social obligation towards the child to preserve his :

'Benignity and home-bred sense
Ripening in perfect innocence'.[3]

Those who fail in such duty are sternly admonished by Chanakya, the Indian savant and political thinker, as being the enemies of the child because untrained boys and girls prove bad face in assemblies, and they look like geese among swans :

माता शत्रु पिता वैंरी ये न वालो न पाठितः ।
न क्षोभते सभामध्ये तेसभध्ये वको यथा ॥[4]

The ancient scripture Satpatha Brahmana laid down an injunction that it is the duty of the mother, father and the teacher to initiate children into truthful knowledge :

मातृमान पितृमान आचार्यवान पुरुषो वेद ।

Continuing this strain the Taittariyopnisad called upon the parents to instruct their children :

यान्यस्माकछ सुचरितानि तानि त्वयोपास्यानि नो इतराणि ॥[5]

"Whatever deeds are blameless, they are to be practised, not others. Whatever good practices there are among us, they are to be adopted by you, not others. And finally the Law giver expressed his highest opinion :

विद्याविलास मनसो धृतशील भिक्षा सत्यमव्रतारहित मानसलापहारः ।
संसार दुख दलनेन सुभूषिता ये धन्या नरा निहितकर्म परोपकारः ॥[6]

A child should grow into a man cultivating knowledge and wisdom, patience, good conduct and truth. He should shun vices, adopt virtues so that he can steer his boat safely in this World. Such a person dedicated to social service and well being of others is really blessed.

3. Wordsworth, William : "To the Highland Girl of Inversneyede."
4. Chanakna : Nitisloka Chap II. Sl 11.
5. Taittariyopnisad : I Section 11, Sl 2.
6. Manusmriti.

Such were the ancient views about children both in the East and the West. But with the rapid rise of Industry and monopolistic economy, children are denuded of their beauty and blossom. Indeed, it is a fall from the sky, yet the Almighty has not denied them His supporting hands, His succour and help. Modern man has his own ways of compensating evil with righteousness, Vice with Virtue, through protective laws against exploitation of human labour. He will discover them as the story unfolds itself step by step through the corridor of time.

Ancient Indian scriptures hardly have any mention of child labour. Instead, children are glorified in the stories of Bharat, Lava, Kush, Dhruva, Prahlad and Nachiketa. There are Aruni, Satyakama Jabala and many others who are commoners, but they are the embodiments of high virtues. We have a number of child prodigies, but we met no child as a social victim in ancient Hindu scriptures. Similarly, each civilised religion, has an approach of glorification towards children for they bring paradise to the Earth, and they are the Gods' good lambs.

But time changes : Tempora mutanture or we may say, like the spokes of a wheel, times favourable and unfavourable go up and down—which is called luck : चक्रारपंक्तिरिव गच्छति भाग्यपंक्तिः ॥[7] The rise of industry brought the fate of children low. Poverty is an unending phenomenon of human history, but the division of man as rich and poor was never so sharp before industrialisation. Industry leads to monopoly and to capitalistic trends, capitalism to plenum dominium (full ownership) or pleonexia (control over as much power as possible) and when capitalism gets mixed up with the alchemy of colonialism, economic menace is colossal. The haves want to acquire weatlh and power from horizon to horizon, they become the Master of the state and use the mechanism of raison d' etat[8] and

7. स्वप्नवासवदत्ता नाटकम् ।
8. *Reson d' etat*—A French word suggesting capture of power by any means.

Real Politik[9] to justify their game of power and plenty, as a consequence of which the havenots live by stooping low, consider slums as their haven, and life long labour as their destiny. How can their children be spared this fate ? Less wages to workers and more profits to investors is managed through child labour and women labour. The will to survive is an impulse pervading this entire world-zoo. Whoever breathes struggles to live : the poor man's battle is deeper and dense for he is luckless. Such a phenomenon is acute even in silk industry. The undeclared war between the employer and the employee goes on in the silk industry of Bhagalpur and to discerning eye, the battle ground leaves a whole gamut of experiences and observations in social fields as much as in the economic areas. The study becomes fruitful because the researcher becomes the spokesman for the mute child whose lot has been to suffer and suffer and yet to take them as a usual way of life—with a sense of acceptence and adjustment rather than rejection and protest.

Silk industry is definitely an ancient industry, although ancient books throw no light on the economic and social aspects involved in its production. China and India both are credited with the breeding of silk worms and making of silk from prehistoric times, "Traditional Chinese accounts ascribe the cultivation of silk worm and the weaving of silk to the wife of the legendery emperor Huang-ti who is supposed to have lived in the third millenium B.C. In any event, silk culture flourished by the time of the Shang dynasty (c. 1523-1027 BC)".[10] "Aristotle and Pliny both describe the silk worm, but for centuries after silk fabrics were known in the West, the prevalent opinion was that silk was either a fleece which grew on a tree, thus confounding it with cotton, or the fibre from the inner bark of some tree or shrub. Some persons, deceived by

9. Real Politik—A German word suggesting that everything is fair in politics.
10. Encyclopeadia Americana, Vol 25, U.S.A. 1918 PI.

the glossy, silky fibers of the seed vessels of Asclepias and the Silk Cotton tree, believed that it was the product of one of these. A few came so near the truth as to conjecture that silk was spun by a spider or beetle. So carefully did the Orient keep its secret that it was not exposed until 552 AD, when two Nestorian monks who had lived in China brought to Constantinople a small quantity of silk worm eggs concealed in their palmer staves".[11]

Silk, therefore, entered Europe via Constantinople. Sericulture spread through the Balkan Peninsula, and, Byzantine silks soon became prized in Europe for ecclesiastical vestments. "Although the looms of Constantinople itself declined in the 8th and 9th Centuries, those of Thebes and other Greeks and Syrian cities increased their production and improved their methods of manufacture. The Greeks maintained their supremacy until 1204, when the Latin Empire was established. Meanwhile the Arabs had introduced the industry into northern Africa, Spain, Portugal, and Sicily. Spanish and Sicilian production was substantial by the 11th century, and when the Norman conquered Sicily (beginning about 1060 AD), they encouraged the local silk industry. The second Norman ruler of Sicily, Roger II (1105-1154), invaded Greece in 1147 and took captive a number of silk weavers whom he established in Palermo and Calabria, where they were induced to teach the Italians Greek methods of silk culture. Venice and Geneva followed Rogers' example in the 13th Century."[12] Rome traded in silk and draped Julius Ceasar in silk garments. Silk industry also flourished in Germany and Switzerland and Belgium right from the Middle Ages.

In India, silk production has a still hoary history. Grita Samad is a Vedic Rishi who lived as a weaver. Weaving wool, silk and cotton was a flourishing profession and had high

11. Ibid.
12. Ibid.

social value. The Rig Veda 10:85:29, while giving away Surya as a bride (daughter of Savitri) mentions : परादेहि शामुल्यं ब्रह्माभ्यो वि भजावसु ।[13]—Put away the woollen robe and make gifts of silken clothes and wealth to the celebrated priests of pure wisdom. In the same strain the Vedic poet says :

> आशसनं विशसनमथो अधिविकर्तनम् ।
> सूर्यायाः पश्य रूपाणि तानि ब्रह्मा तु शुन्धति ।।[14]

Weaving was mostly home industry, managed by women generally. The Rig Veda II, 3,6 : II, 38,4 etc. explicitly mention the importance of warp and woof in weaving industry. It was a trade dedicated to the Lord Pushan that is the God of social nourishment.[15] Elaborating on the process of weaving, the Rig Veda mentions Weaver as Vaya (RV-X, 26,6) the loom as Vaman. "The shuttle used for weaving called lesara. The warp was called Otu and the woof tanta (VI, 5,2). Weaving was generally left to women (I, 92,3)". Gradually, the society gave the name of Tantuvay, Tanti, Tatva to the weaver community based on the word Tanta or the Yarn. Modern Bhagalpur has the largest number of Tantis (Hindu weavers) who live on weaving silk and, staple and pleasantly enough there are equal number of Momins or Julahas (Muslim weavers who weave and sell silk).

Silk finds a place of honour in the Epics too. Devi Sita and Shree Rama are married and the bridegroom party is ready

13. Rig Veda 10:85:29—See Hymns from the Vedas by A.C. Bose, Asia Publishing House, Calcutta, 1965, p. 134.
14. Rig Veda 10:85:35, ibid.
    Look at the most beautiful bride Surya. Look at her beautiful silken border cloth and her head apparel. Her garment is triply parted and these have been sanctified by the revered priest.
15. Refer to R.C. Dutta—'Early Hindu Civilization' Punthi Pustak, Calcutta 1963, p. 39 and Radha Kumud Mukherjee "Hindu Civilization" Bhartiya Vidya Bhavan, Bombay 1950 p. 75.

to go back to Ayodhya with the brides. The King of Mithila, Raja Janaka offers to King Desoratha :

गवां शतसहस्त्राणि वद्दनि मिथिलेश्वरः ।
कम्बलानां च मुख्यानां क्षोभान् कोट त्राम्वराणि च ।।
दृसियश्व च रथयारातं दिव्यरूपेम् स्वलंकृतम् ।।4।।[16]

We meet Devi Sita again in Valmiki's Sunderkand. Sri Hanuman has found her in Ashok Vatika and is extremely affected by the sight :

पीतनैकेन संवीतां क्लिष्ठनोत्तम वाससा ।
स षङ्कामनलंकारा विपदभामिव पद्मिनीम् ।।29।।[17]

Yet again in Sunderkanda, Hanuman asks the Devi about herself :

का नु पद्म परपासाक्षि क्लिस्ठुकौशेय वासिनी ।
द्रुमस्य शाखामालम्ब्य तिष्ठसि त्वमनिन्दिते ।। 3 ।।[18]

Sri Hanuman repeats this episode to Bharat, while narrating to him how he discovered Devi Sita in Ravan's custody in Ashok Vatika :

कौशेय वस्त्रां मलिनां मिरानन्दाम् दृढ़व्रताम् ।।[19]

16. *Valmiki Ramayana*—Geeta Press, Balkand,
At the time of farewell Raja Janaka made great presentation viz. thousand of Cows, Carpets, Silk dress, Cotton pieces and well bedecked elephants, horses, chariots and infantry.

17. *Valmiki Ramayana*—Sunderkand—Gita Press, verse 21 Sita looked a picture of sorrow and gloom dressed in an old and Tattered yellow silk dress. She seemed like a muddy pond bereft of lotus.

18. Ibid, p. 945.
Who are you Lotus eyed lady, dressed in a worn out silk apparel and standing taking help of the trees' trunk ?

19. Ibid, Yuddhakanda—p. 1440 Ver : 44
Devi Sita wore a tattered silk sari and looked devoid of the spirit of hope, but steadfast in her love for her Lord Rama.

In the Mahabharata, Lord Krishna looms large over the whole epic as Pitambar (पीताम्बर) or clad in yellow silken robes. All the Princes and Princesses in the Mahabharata wear silk as उवृटीय, शृंङ्गावस्त्रम् etc. Later history informs us of a flourishing trade between India, Bactria, Scythia, Greece and Rome in silk as in other commodities. The Hindu Kings, and priests and affluent commoners used silk not only for its purity, but as a mark of status. This continued even during the Mughal rule. That silk rearing with its worms and cocoons was too common in the Indian social life is revealed from a Doha (दोहा) of the great poet Tulsidas :

पन्नगारि असि नीति श्रुति संमत सज्जन कहहिं ।
अति नीचहुं सन प्रीति करिअ जानि निज परमहित ॥
पाट कीट ते होई तेहि ते पाटम्बर रुचिर ।
कृमि पालई सब कोई परम अयावन प्रान सम ॥ 5 ख ॥[20]

As time progresses, Indian history takes a sharp turn. Europeans arrive on the Indian soil through its waters and when confronted by Zamorin of Calicut, they say that they have come in search of silk, saltpetre, spices and christians. Silk is one of their attractions in India as a commodity of trade. Let us have a look at the different directives issued by them to secure silk and parcel them off to England and other countries of the west.

The East India Company was enamoured of silk trade and the enormous profits accruing from it. There are numerous references to the making of silk, from worm rearing to weaving, dyeing and finally to export. Right from the establishment of the East India Company, that is in the period 1650-1657, we

20. *Ramcharitamanasa* : Uttarkand : years 95 K & Kh Kakbhusundi speaks to Garudji 'The Vedas and the sages say that one should love the lowliest person for love glorifies man. For example, silk is made out of worms which is a lowly creature, but it begets the raiment which every man loves.

have on record clearcut instructions about the procurement of silk for despatch to England. Particular orders were issued in this regard 'commending the example of the Dutch for irnitation. It was clearly laid down "In silke you know what great matters are to be done, therefore it doth import the Company much, that you strive both by relation and your own experience to know how, and where best to carry on the manufacture thereof, where the best silkes are procured, and where the best conveniences are for fitting and preparing the same for the sale, of Europe, that so if the Company shall require large quantities you may be in a posture to fit them all the first hand. I suppose the order of the Dutch is very good, and will be freest from adulteration, the properest way will be to make three sorts, as Head, Belly, and foote, each apart by themselves. You may also make an experience of washing thereof at Hukely or elsewhere, and send the Company a maund of each sort apart by the next shipping for a sample, with an exact account of the loss in washing, and charge of the same. In this commodity you may invest neare three eight parts of your remaines."[21]

Considering the rich prospects of silk exports, the East India Company took note of the "defects in the native manner of preparing it". "The court objected to the vicious practice of dyeing it in the gum, and as early as 1663 asked that the taffetas should be brought in the ungummed state as they could receive this improvement in England in a superior manner, a successful experiment having been tried which made the Bengal silks pass in the market as Italian".[22] Later some skilled artisans in dyeing were sent to India with clear instructions to keep their art a secret. This helped the silk trade in England increase four fold. Cassimbazar, Hugli, Patna and Agra were the important silk marts, but "Cassimbazar, was the head-

21. Wilson, C.R. The Early Annals of the English in Bengal, Vol I, Bimla Publishing House, New Delhi, Reprinted 1988, p. 26.
22. Ibid., p. 46.

quarters of the silk trade and was almost equal in importance to Hugli....All the district round was planted with mulberry trees, the young leaves being in great request for feeding the silk worms. The silk itself was yellow, like most crude silks, but the people of Cassimbazar knew how to bleach it with a lye made of the ashes of the plantain tree, which made it as white as the silk of Palestine".[23] Patna silk used to sell from Rs. $5\frac{1}{2}$ to $6\frac{1}{2}$ per seer, a costly affair indeed in those times, because the quality was fine and worth purchasing. Warehousing of silk and its accounts keeping were meticulous and thorough as recorded in the early annals. The trade was so brisk that on 2nd May 1714 The Hon'ble Company directed that "no Person in Calcutta have liberty to export till the Company have the refusall,"[24] which means that there was the end of *laissez faire* system of trade in silk and monopolistic trends were strictly adhered to by the East India Company.

By the turn of the Century the East India Company was always in search of free trade permission from the Mogul overlord. Luxury and licentiousness had overtaken the last of the Moghul Emperors, and to satisfy their impulses accepting bribes in the form of gifts and presentations was the most convenient way. The historians of the East India Company have placed on record the grim consequences which India was to face, and the advantages that would go to the Company for trifles. "The mention of presents consisting of cloth, silk and brocades, fire-arms, spirits and perfumes, glassware, clockwork and other toys, appears to have aroused the curiosity of the Imperial Court, for in such matters Farruskhsiyar was little better than a child and it appears to have been thought quite worthwhile to gratify the English at Calcutta with an order for freedom of trade, if only this wonderful present could br

23. Ibid., p. 55 (Taken from Hedges' Diary II 236 and Taverniers Voyages, Vol. II p. 261, Paris edition of (1677).
24. Ibid., Vol, II, P I, p. 217.

brought to Delhi".[25] And the presents of "Silks and cloth, arms, clocks and toys, two Japanese Copper fountains and a double-barrelled gun and finally fifty more chests of shiraz wine" did their magic on the Emperor, and his court, for on all counts the presents weighed sixty tons of delightful items.[26] For this purpose, in October 1713, orders were received in Calcutta under the seal of Taqarrub Khan, the lord Steward, who directed the Governors of Bengal, Patna, Allahabad, and Akbarabad to guard the presents through their several governments till its arrival with the English embassy at Court. The Company got in return what it wanted—permission for free trade in Bengal.

But this was not the end of the British agony in matters of silk trade. They had fierce competition with the Dutch, French and other European Communities struggling to find their foothold in India. Sagacity and skill were on the side of the Englishmen if not actual fire power until the arrival of Clive at Plassey. We come across a despatch dated Monday, February 13th, 1721 as under :

"This being the proper season for providing the November Bund Silk, and to have the silk piece goods made of the same, which is not to be had if not timely bespoke, besides we hearing the French design immediately to send up People to Cassimbazar to settle their factory there, which will of course make all goods or rise in price, wherefore.

Agreed we immediately write up to Mr. John Deare & Co. and order them to contact for the following goods being according to the list of investment received from the Hon. Court of Directors by the last ships, viz.

25. Wilson, C.R., *The Early Annals of the English in Bengal*, Vol, II Part II, P IX.

26. Ibid., pp. XIV & XX.

Raw silk November Bund	600 mds
Silk Lungi Romalls	4000 pieces"[27]

They fixed their price carefully keeping the market rate of French in mind.

"Raw silk Nov' Bund—600 mds@ Rs. 4.12 as per seer
Silk Lungi Romalls —5000 @ 5/- per seer[28] and so on.

The mention of Bhagalpur silk separately is not possible during the period under consideration for all this area came under Bengal, and Bhagalpur manufactures flowed down the Ganges to Cossimbazar or up stream to Patna. But Bhagalpur had a flourishing trade of silk manufacture as we shall see in the records of the century just following, that is the 19th century. That Bhagalpur pargana was a part of Bengal subah in those times, we may collect from Major Renneli's map of the "Jungleterry District published in 1779 as Plate II of his Bengal Atlas". Along with it must be read Rennell's statistics of "Area of the Bengal Provinces". There "Monghir (modern Monghyr) is shown containing 8,270 Sq. miles, and,

(a) Baglipour (modern Bhagalpur) 2817 Sq. m.
(b) Curruckpour (Kharagpur) 2696 Sq. m. etc."[29]

Bhagalpur silk worms rearing is definitely an ancient industry. Writing about 250 years back the East India Company Surveyor whose reports have been collected from the original documents preserved in the East India House, London, by Montgomery Martin, it is mentioned that "In the estimate, what is called silk, consists often of the Maldehi cloth, made

27. Wilson, C.R., *The Early Annals of the English in Bengal* Vol III, p. 319.
28. Ibid., p. 322.
29. Taken from the Journal of Francis Buchanan (kept during the survey of the District of Bhagalpur in 1810-1811) Prepared by E.A.W. Oldham C.S.I.I.C.S. (Retd.) Government Press, Patna 1930, p. XI (Introduction).

of silk and cotton mixed."[30] This silk especially Tasar silk is produced with the help of worm on a tree. "The tree abounds chiefly in the part of the district that is situated east from the Chandan, and between that and the Rajmahal hills, and there occupies as large space as the bamboo does towards the west. The animal reared by all castes, who inhabit these parts, but in general by the armed man employed under Ghatwals to preserve the peace of the country".[31] Giving further details the author goes on to say : "Concerning the method of procuring the seed cocoons, I found in the accounts of the natives the utmost differences. In Bangka (Banka—modern) it was stated, that the only good seed was procured from the forests, from whence the spontaneous Cocoons were brought by people of wild tribes, were purchased by merchants and distributed among those who rear the worm. From the Cocoons three successive breeds are reared, but those reared from the wild cocoons (Dhaba) are the best, the others Sarihan, Jarhan and Langa, gradually degenerate. At Tarapoor and Lakardewani it was stated that the kinds are quite distinct, that the good Tasar (Dhaba) is always reared from cultivated cocoons, some of which are preserved through the year for propagating the breed, and that the wild cocoons are only used for this purpose, when from accident or carcless-ness the proper seed is lost, and the Tasar, which these give, is always of an inferior quality, 'but is of two kinds, Sarihan and Langa, the last of which is very inferior, and is seldom employed. Each kind, according to these people breeds twice in the year...The weavers indeed say, that there is a difference in the quality of cocoons, and that one kind (Dhaba) is more easily wound, and gives a larger quantity of silk, while the Sarihan produces $\frac{1}{4}$ less, but it is of better quality. The merchants who deal with the simple breeders endeavour probably to keep up distinctions, of which they avail

30. Martin, Montgumery, *Eastern India* Vol II, Delhi, 1976, p. 93.
31. Ibid., p. 157.

themselves. They pay in advance for the whole, and give a very low price, but they no doubt are often defrauded by people who never fulfil their engagements".[32]

The surveyor has indeed collected some romantic tales of the silk worm which are interesting as well as informative. To impress the people about the purity of silk that is easily given a place of honour in Hindu worships, "it is supposed (and also believed) that a Tasar female moth will not admit the embraces of a male of the same paternal family with herself. The breeders however very judiciously leave the whole adjustment of this delicate point to the discretian of the females. The seed cocoons are placed on a large flat basket ; and when the moths burst the cocoons, they are allowed to form such connections as they please. In from 15 to 20 hours the males are thrown away, and from 20 to 25 impregnated females are placed in a cylindrical basket with a narrow mouth, which is covered with leaves, and some leaves are laid on the bottom of the basket. In some places an earthen pot is preferred. On these leaves, in the course of the day, the females deposit their eggs, and are then thrown away, and the eggs are placed in small baskets made of the Bhela leaves. On the ninth day afterwards the eggs are hatched, and the baskets on which they are lying are put upon a tree, over the leaves of which the young insects immediately spread. When they have consumed these, the worms are removed to other trees, and in 36 days from being hatched they begin to spin. In 15 days this operation is completed, when all the young branches are cut, and the cocoons are thus collected with very little trouble....The worms however must be watched, as crows and other birds and hornets apt to destroy them. The whole space of time occupied by the two crops may be about 5 months, beginning about the first of July, and ending about the last of November. A great number of the cocoons preserved for seed burst, and these can only be sold for about

32. Ibid., pp. 157-158.

half price. Those originally intended for sale are killed by being put in boiling water, and then dried in the Sun."

"In procuring food for these worms, the only trouble is to select a piece of ground on which the Asan tree grows, intermixed with few others. These latter, and all bushes ought to be removed, and all the large branches of the asan tree should be lopped near the stem, and young shoots permitted to grow : for these produce large succulent leaves fit for the worm. The worms are only applied to the same tree once in the two years, a whole year being necessary to allow the new shoot to grow."[33]

Dyeing silk, like dyeing cotton, was quite prevalent in Bhagalpur. Fascinating colour, like the 'pomegranate red (Sorukh or Kusami), green or sabza, 'Golabi' or rose, Naranggi' or orange colour and 'Zurd' or yellow of different shades were commonly used. Dyes were extracted from diverse flowers, mixed with fruit juice or acid and we may read in detail about these in the survey reports alluded to.[34] "Kakreja'—a Dark brown colour inclining towards purple, 'Agari' (a brown without any tinge of purple) "Uda"—a bright purplish brown 'Habasi' or blood-red colour, 'Baygani (approaching claret colour) or violet, 'Asmani', a light sky blue, 'Torunji'—a bright gambage yellow, 'Fakhtah'—a bluish ash colour, and 'Shishaha', a pale blue compared to lead, were the attractions of coloured silk. The Bhagalpur colour on silk was always fast and excellent and smooth. The surveyor mentions : "The dyers of Bhagalpur partly give the same colours ; but about 12 hours are constantly employed in dyeing the mixed cloth made of cotton and Tasar silk, which is woven in the vicinity of that town. These dyers give a colour to pieces that are of an uniform colour (Baftahs) and that are dyed after having been woven."[35]

33. Ibid., pp. 158-159.
34. Ibid., refer pages 267-271.
35. Ibid., p. 269.

There were about 3275 looms working in the beginning of the 19th century in Bhagalpur. In modern times "A Government Dye house has been started at Nathnagar to provide facilities to the weaver at Nathnagar and Champanagar in getting their yarns dyed at a reasonable fixed rate."[36] With the growth of silk exports from Bhagalpur, in Independent India weaving dyeing have become cottage industries, especially with the advent of powerlooms replacing handlooms, which invite the cooperation of the entire family to this trade in order to boost profits.

Bhagalpur deals in the four kinds of popular silk, viz. Eri, Tassar, Mulberry and Moonga, although the last one is brought from outside yet weaving is done at Bhagalpur. Winding of the threads is an important part of the job and is done equally by men and women. As already stated the whole business of producing silk is not only a cottage industry but family employment. Writing in the 19th century the Surveyor observed :

"A woman takes five 'Pans' of cocoons (405) and puts them in a large earthen pot with 600 sicca weight of water' a small mat being placed in the bottom to prevent the cocoons from being burnt. A small quantity of pot ash, tied in a bit of cloth, is put into the pot, along with the cocoons, which are boiled for about an European hour. They are then cooled, the water is then changed, and they are again boiled. The water is poured off, and the cocoons are put into another pot, where they stand three days, in the sun covered with a cloth to exclude insects. On the fourth day they are again boiled, with 200 picea weight of water, for rather less than an hour, and then poured into a basket, where they are allowed to cool, after which they are washed in cold water, and placed to dry on a layer of cow-dung ashes, where they remain spread

36. Bihar District Gazeteer (Bhagalpur) 1962, p. 247.

and covered with a cloth for six hours. The woman then picks out such cocoons as are not quite ready, for winding and exposes them for a day or two to the sun, which completes the operation. The outer filaments of the cocoon are then picked off, and form a substance called Jhuri, of which the potters make brushes used for applying a pigment to their vessels. The fibres from 4 to 5 cocoons are then wound off on a miserable conical real (below) which is twisted round by one hand, while the thread is twisted on the thigh, the cocoons adjusted, and the broken fibres joined by the other....This thread is called Lak, and after the Lak has been removed, there remains another inferior kind of filament, called also Jhuri, which is wound off, and is purchased by those, who knit strings".[37] What the author seems to consider Jhuri as a silk product of inferior kind is, in modern times, a rich product earning foreign money through bulk export from Bhagalpur. Of course, among the four types of cloth woven locally are the Duriyas (cotton and tassar mixed), Namunahs (also cotton and Tasar mixed). Baftah—a speciality of Bhagalpur and finally Khariasari. Baftah inspite of its glossiness, its peculiar dye, strength and attraction is on the declining scale if compared to Jhuri on the one hand and staple products on the other. Sutrunji, bedsheets, pillow cover, lungi and wrappers are more on the market list than the precious Bhagalpuri Baftah.

37. Ibid., pp. 272-273. Also see *Bhagalpur Gazetteer*, p. 228 "Under the head of Tassar can be considered Bafta or mixed cloths. This is associated with Bhagalpur".

While the Government of India is quite aware of a growing slump in silk industry, it is trying its level best to give it a fillip and thus help the tribal people, the Adivasis, and the weaver community widely scattered all over Bhagalpur Division, against economic annihilation. It has therefore started "Six ERI Demonstration Centres at Birpur, Naugachia, Gopalpur, Pirpainty, Sabour and Akbarnagar. Disease-free layings are distributed among the villagers free of cost and cocoons are purchased from rearers on cash payment by the Government Silk Institute, Nathnagar. At Katoria a Tassar seed supply sub-station has been started to supply disease free layings of tassar to the rearers."

The State Government has sanctioned a scheme of introducing 150 powerlooms. The uumber of powerlooms in Nathnagar and Champanagar has increased a hundred fold with liberal grant-in-aid from the Bihar Government in order to encourage the weavers concentrated at Nathnagar and Champanagar. Each loanee of powerlooms will be given an advance of Rs. 1000/- as working capital repapable in five annual instalments."[38]

But this is not the end of the woes of silk weavers. There has been an invasion of nylon and other synthetic fibres which make a cloth lasting, tenascious, easily washable and preservable and in so many shades and colours that easily outwit purchasers or manufactuers of silk. This invasion is universal like a world war on silk. Military necessities have encouraged synthetic fibres cloth both for defensive and offensive purposes, as well as enchanting raiments. In USA "by 1933, the silk industry had become a silk rayon industry, and in that year the name of the Silk Association of America was changed to the National Federation of Textiles, Inc. By the end of 1939, only 9% of the raw silk imports were used by fabric manufacturers.

38. *Gazetteer of India*, Bihar, District of Bhagalpur, Secretariat Press, Bihar, Patna 1962, p. 247.

The consumption of silk by the hosiery industry was still high but in 1940 nylon was introduced in this manufacture. In 1941, when war with Japan cut off the shipment of raw silk from the orient, silk was almost eliminated from the United States market?"[39]

The post war conditions were damaging to silk industry in USA. When World War II ended in 1945, the textile industry anticipated the return of Japanese raw silk and expected that consumption would be renewed at the 1939 level, and at prices equal to those of the late 1920's. A market research survey was then conducted by Weavers and Knitters to learn why silk was not more popular. They discovered that consumers had become accustomed to improved man made fibers during the war ; manufacturing from raw silk had became difficult and costly because most of the machineries had been replaced by those employing rayon and nylon. The automatic loom was more suited to produce synthetic cloth in place of silk cloth ; workers had become adapted to changed circumstances, and pay bases of labourers had become determined on the new power looms. Silk power looms had become diminished to 3,328 in 1950 which were 100,000 in 1930.

Yet, silk remains a fancy and a taste of elites today as much as in the days of yore. Its revival was a natural demand. The appeal of silk was never dead or outdated. Steadily, silk industry started picking up. "According to the United States Bureau of the Census, 22.1 million yards of silk fabrics were produced in 1950" which was a shortfall as compared to 1930 or 1939 figures, yet it was a definite symptom of revival because the silk units had started breathing again. To catch up a market, USA tried its hands on imports also, which signify that the American Citizen loved to wear and use silk in all its manifestations. What the World War II had brought to USA in the sphere of silk industry as a windfall, had also been

39. *Encyclopaedia Americana*, op. cit., Silk andthe Silk and Industry p. 3.

witnessed in India in those days. Silk industry awaits its resuscitation in India too as in many other countries, because the invasion of synthetic fibres was like a Mongol onslaught that left only devastation and ruin in its trail. But revival of silk industry is as much a social necessity as historical, and it has come in India with its government allocating Rs. 510 crores with the aid of the World Bank and the target of silk production has been raised from 9,000 metric tonnes to 16,000 metric tonnes annually. Bihar gets about Rs. 150/- crores out of the proposed allocation for India. The Chairman, Central Silk Board (India) told newsmen that "considering the importance of sericulture as a rural based cottage industry and its capacity to generate employment opportunities and improve village economy both the Union Government and State Governments have been paying more attention for development of the sericulture industry. As non-mulberry sericulture is mainly practised by the tribals, efforts are being made to further expand and develop non-mulberry sericulture industry".

"Mr. Muniraju said around 1,26,000 tribals are engaged in tassar silkworm rearing and production of cocoons in different states, around 460 metric tonnes of tassar raw silk is being produced per annum and Bihar is the major tassar silk producing state".

"The proudction of tassar has remained stagnant. Similarly the other varieties of non-mulberry silk like Eri and Muga are produced by the tribals particularly in north eastern region. The muga silk production has been declining in recent years."

"The Chairman said among the many reasons which hamper its development, the depletion of silkworm food plants near the tribal villages has been one of the main constraints".

"The committee, has therefore, suggested raising of food plants of tassar, eri, and muga in concentrated patches on government wastelands, panchayat lands, and forest areas and allotting them to the tribals to carry out the silkworm rearing activity".

"He said certain percentage of plantation raised under social forestry programme and wasteland development programme should be reserved exclusively for raising of silkworm food plants. In the Seventh Plan it was proposed to implement projects for intensive development of topical tassar, oak tassar, muga and eri silk industry.... In the eighth plan period it was proposed to set up Tassar silk worm seed rearing units in tribal areas in different states...."

Further the Chairman said that "towards marketing of Tassar, muga and eri silk cocoons produced by the tribals, it was proposed to develop proper marketing organisation by associating the Tribal Cooperative Marketing Development Federation of India (TRIFED) and a Committee is being constituted to work out suitable schemes for purchasing the cocoons directly from primary producers at a reasonable price and to organise its inter state sales as also export thus preventing the exploitation of tribals by private traders and middlemen."[40]

Silk industry beginning from the life cycle of silk worms, its special food of particular leaves, the plantation of such trees and their cyclic preservation, then the rearing of silkworm through various stages, the production of silk fibres and cloth, their gumming, dyeing, polishing and finishing into brilliant shades and colours after calendering (Kundi style as well) and finally the earning of revenue through internal consumption and exports, make a fascinating study of the intimate relationship of man and Nature. It naturally entails intensive study of Natural History, social and economic impacts of silk industry. The production of silk brings into bold relief the

40. Morning News Bull:tin, All India Radio, Delhi and TV transmission on National Network on 13-3-89 and Times of India, Patna Edition, Monday March 13, 1989.

participation of both the family child and child on hire as essential labour or an integral part of silk production. Naturally an interaction of labour and industry and profits necessitate the stepping in of legislative reforms where and whenever required. Industry is not all gold : it creates disabilities in society, like exploitation, inequality and rebellion. All these shall be our concern hereafter since silk industry is no exception. Meanwhile, we may interest ourselves in the ups and downs which silk industry has faced over the past years from times immemorial, and modern resurgence in the sphere of silk production.

CHAPTER III

Child Labour : Prevalence in India as Cheap Human Resource

To produce a yard of silk entails passing through a hundred odd jobs—say, from rearing plants and cocoons to reeling of silk yarns, dyeing, starching, drying and straightening before putting them as warp and weft on handlooms or powerlooms. Being primarily a cottage industry or a small scale industry at Bhagalpur particularly, children contribute significantly towards silk manufacture. The essential participation of children into the manufacture brings into bold relief the problem of child labour along with its social, economic and legal implications. Whether all such participations are to be treated as legally prohibited 'child labour', or some cases can be passed off as vocational training or voluntary assistance towards improving family income, deserve to be distinguished on merit. Primarily therefore, we have to discuss what is 'child labour'—a reprehensible and punishable act, and what makes a similar labour voluntary assistance and a welcome effort to augment family income.

Decidedly, all labour is not exploitation, and therefore should not be decried. Ancient Indian savants and teachers called upon the initiates into the Ashram to contribute their 'Shram' (श्रम) or labour to'Goraksha', 'Krishi' and Paricharya, apart from textual study, recitation and meditation. These would never come under the purview of harsh or cruel labour. When 'Gandhiji', Vinoba Bhave, Dr. Zakir Husain and Sri Aryanayakam introduced Basic Education under Wardha Training Scheme and called upon young boys and girls to take up vocational training by using their limbs as a means of preparing for future life, then such labour-based training was not an exploitation. It was, instead, a training in self dependence and dignity of labour. But these Ashram ideals were swept away as India moved speedily towards industrialisation. Monopoly and urbanisation grow with modern technical industry and bring in its wake an unquenchable spirit of profiteering. Cheap child labour is an unfailing aid to high profiteering. Thus, we can differentiate between simple labour-amateurish in tone and spirit, and harsh exploitation of child labour. Rightly does the eminent author say : "The basic attributes of work are purpose, plan and freedom : when they are conspicuously absent work becomes labour. Labour in the case of the child especially, is harmful because the energy that should have been expended on the nurturing of his latent powers is consumed for purposes of bare survival. Child labour assumes the character of a social problem in as much as it hinders, arrests, or distorts the natural growth procvsses and prevents the child from attaining his fully blown manhood."[1] Further, it is said, "when the business of wage earning or of participation in self or family support conflicts directly or indirectly with the basiness of growth and education, the result is child labour. The function of work in childhood is primarily developmental and not economic. Childrcn's work then as a social good is the direct antithesis of child

1. Report on the Committee on Child Labour, Nasik, Government of India Press, 1981, p. 8.

labour as a social evil."[2] Work by its nature is enriching : forced labour by its circumstances is depleting and deleterious.

Labour becomes nefarious when it is ultimately against the interests of the labourer—physical, mental or moral. In the case of the child it is absolutely evil "when he is required to work beyond his physical capacity, when hours of work interfere with his education, recreation and rest, when his wages are not commensurate with the quantum of work done, and when the occupation he is engaged in endangers his health and safety, i.e., then he is exploited."[3] By a child's exploitation in the field of labour, we actually mean the exploitation of human values, the perpetuation of social evil, the childs exposure to dangers and job risks, his being deprived of desirable opportunities of life, and in the last analysis, his being utilised for selfish gains better called profiteering. But here rises a pertinent question. What compel a child to join the labour force where he has to work like a mute animal ? Who compels him, and when is he compelled ? Social analysts have given their attention to this positively harmful aspect, and the government, both in the States, and at the Centre, have expressed their deep concern at the baneful effects of child labour. Hence, it will be prudent for us to find out the causes of child labour—its why, when and how.

First, traditionally, children of the upper caste families begin their lives in schools, according to their affluence and taste, whereas children of the have-nots begin their lives in work culture, in their own families. Gaining a little skill and sturdiness, they move out in search of work and wages, while their higher aspirations get "fossilised". Hence traditional illiteracy paves the way to child labour.

Secondly, nearly half of India's population lives below the poverty line. The rural scene is deplorable. Chronic poverty

2. *Encyclopaedia of Social Sciences*, Vol. 3. p. 412.
3. Report of the Committee on Child Labour, op. cit., p. 8.

stalks in the face of agricultural tenants and labourers who consider children's education a luxury. Parents look at their children as those born with economic compulsions. The income accrued from child labour mny be a pittance but it plays a crucial role in saving the family from ruin. Economic compulsions weigh heavily on the consciousness of poor parents who will not fight shy of colluding with the employers and violate all laws. They would not shirk from forcing their children to undergo inhuman labour, if it adds to their family income. Education and better upbringing are dream objects while poverty and deprivation are real.

Thirdly, the choice of the employers. They prefer children to adults. Employers find children without ego, without status-consciousness and more amenable to discipline and control. In running errands, children do better than adults. They are quick and agile of limb when compared to adults.

Fourthly, the greatest menace for employers is trade union, and the children have none. They submit silently to the excesses of their masters which we can collect from numerous English novels written after the Industrial Revolution in Europe. Notwithstanding the outrageoues scenes depicted therein, the employees too have some logic that sustains preference for child labour. "The National Commission on Labour (1969) found that it was the feeling of sympathy rather than the desire to exploit which weighed with some children's employers Instead of condemnation, they expected commendation from society for their benevolent act of saving the child from starvation and waywardness. Then there are crafts (zari brocade work for example) in which highest degree of sophistication and excellence cannot be achieved unless learning is initiated in childhood itself. No fineness can be acquired if the fingers have lost their suppleness and have become stiff at the time of initiation. Child labour is thus justified on the ground that it trains the child's fingers in the required skill. Unless the fingers were trained at a very early age their adaptation later would be difficult. A similar logic is advanced for children engaged in acrobatics and circuses."[4]

Fifthly, in villlages non-schooling of children and child labour go together. "Of the 547,672 villages in the country, as many as 48,566 do not have schools and 167,382 rural schools are functioning with just one teacher apiece." Even where they are, the schools present a drab and dismal picture, abhorrent rather then attractive. Time and necessity both call for jobs and the children are easily harnessed to them to make their lives worthwhile.

To sum up, therefore, the report on child labour informs : "Working children (200) in Madras, advanced the following reasons for seeking employment :

To supplement family income (72.5%), death of the father (23%), do not like to depend on others (19%), parents asked to search for jobs (17%), for out of pocket expenses (10%), no one to look after (7%), no other earning member (5%), to earn for education (5%) to learn to job (4%), asked to assist in occupation (3%), was interested in the job (3%), just to escape attending school (0.4%)."[5] In addition to this, we have more information from Bombay that reveal the causes of child labour. Parents of working children in Bombay (287) narrated the following circumstantial reasons for sending their children to work, viz, child labour is our family tradition (41%), the child has left school (24.0%) he was having bad company/ getting delinquent (6%), death/disease/loss of job of the earning member (21%), economic compulsions (59.2%), child wanted to earn (4.1%), child was idle and doing nothing (25.8%), child was alone at home and not safe (1%)."[6] Likewise a

4. Ibid., pp. 10-11.
5. George, K.N. "Child Labour in the city of Madras". A paper presented at the National Seminar on Employment of Child in India, 1975.
6. 'Working Children in Bombay', National Institute of Public Cooperation and Child Development, New Delhi 1978. (Quoted in the Report on the Committee on Child Labour, p. 12).

Research Report by the Indian Council for Child Welfare informs us about the Union Territory of Delhi ; "Assuming an estimated population of 38.5 lakhs in mid 1972, the labour force would amount to 13.96 lakhs. Children below the age of 14, accounted for 1.5% of the labour force ; the estimated number of child labour force thus comes to about 22,000."[7] This figure relates to state sector study of 240 urban blocks only. The magnitude of the problem of child labour can be understood from a Report of the Director General of International Labour Organization Pt I, 1960, who tells us regarding country :

"In respect of India, about a third of the 10 to 14 years old children in rural areas and an eighth of those in urban areas are at work".

The Report IV (I) of the 57th Session of Internatioual Labour Conference, Geneva, 1972, indicates that "90% or more of the child population is engaged in the employment market in the developing regions of the world. The report has also indicated that 41, 125,000 children, making 5.1% of the whole of 0-14 age group were engaged in 1960 and in 1970, the number was reduced to 39,975,000 which formed 4% of the children. In the industrialised area the number of child workers in the year 1960 was 4,095,000 which formed 1.4% of all children and in 1970 the number was 3,343,000 constituting 1.1% of the total children".[8] As against this scene obtaining in the developing countries, the Indian census held in 1971 report that 10.7 million children were engaged in employment in India. "Out of them only 0.7 million, constituting 7% were working in urban areas, and the remaining 10 million i.e. 93% were rmployed in rural areas.78.7% of the child labour was employed as cultivators and agricultural labourers. The remaining 8.2% were employed

7. 'Working Children in Urban Delhi' : Report submitted to the Deptt. of Social Welfare, Government of India, 1977, p. 6-7.
8. Kulshreshtha, J.C. : Child Labour in India, Ashish Publishing House, New Delhi, 1978, p. 3.

livestock, forestry, fishing, hunting, plantation and orchards, etc. 6.1% in household and other industries and 2.4% in trade, commerce, transport, storage and communication and rest in construction, mining and other services."[9] The soreid scene of child labour in urban areas has been prompted by urbanisation as a consequence of industrialisation meaning thereby, masss exodus of families from rural areas to towns in search bread and of better living. How much has this been accomplished is a matter of imagination, still migration from villages to cities is endlessly continuing.

Since we have studied in brief the causes of child labour in India as also in the developing countries, we will be profitted by a study of the main areas where they are employed. Perhaps there is no sphere where children are not visible labouring and producing for the profit of the employers. Exploitation of child is rampant even inspite of stringent consitutional measures againat this undesirable practice. The following state-wise figures are indeed revealing about the enormity of the problem of child exploitation :

1981 Census of Indian Child Labourers (in thousands)[10].

1	*2*
Andhra Pradesh	1754
Arunachal Pradesh	14
Bihar	893
Gujarat	462
Haryana	142
Himachal Pradesh	60
Jammu & Kasnmir	109
Karnataka	966

(Contd.)

9. Ibid., p. 4.
10. The Hindustan Times, Patna, Tuesday, Nov. 15, 1988.

1	2
Kerala	68
Madhya Pradesh	1372
Maharashtra	1263
Manipur	17
Meghalaya	39
Nagaland	14
Orissa	515
Punjab	179
Rajasthan	589
Sikkim	7
Tamil Nadu	871
Tripura	19
Uttar Pradesh	1246
West Bengal	523
Andaman & Nicobar Island	1
Chandigarh	1
Dadra & Nagar Haveli	2
Delhi	24
Mizoram	31
Pondicherry	3

The percentage of total workers i.e., main workers and marginal workers among children in the age group O-14 for persons according to 1981 census, is given on next page for India in general and all states and union territories in particular (UTs) except Assam and the states of Andhra Pradesh, Orissa and Tamil Nadu for which 1971 census have been taken into consideration. These are reflected as fallows :

Percentage of Total Workers Among Children for India/States/UTs 1981 Census.[11]

India/States/UTs		*Percentage of total workers among children*		
		P	*M*	*F*
1	*2*	*3*	*4*	*5*
INDIA		5.17	5.96	4.32
States :				
1.	Bihar*	3.74	4.87	2.52
2.	Gujarat*	4.70	5.27	4.09
3.	Haryana*	3.61	4.47	2.65
4.	Himachal Pradesh	5.88	4.66	7.14
5.	Jammu & Kashmir	10.53	10.48	10.58
6.	Karnataka*	7.64	8.74	6.52
7.	Kerala*	1.08	1.10	1.06
8.	Madhya Pradesh*	7.90	8.24	7.54
9.	Maharashtra*	6.42	6.18	6.67
10.	Manipur	3.62	2.88	4.37
11.	Meghalaya	7.92	8.85	6.99
12.	Nagaland	5.69	5.01	6.39
13.	Punjab*	3.62	5.67	1.32
14.	Rajasthan*	5.64	6.00	5.27
15.	Sikkim	6.83	5.75	7.96
16.	Tripura	3.00	3.88	2.09
17.	Uttar Pradesh*	3.04	4.50	1.37
18.	West Bengal*	2.83	4.34	1.27

11. *Social Welfare*, Vol. XXXIII, May 1986, 2 p. 2,

Union Territories

1	2	*3*	*4*	*5*
1.	Andaman & Nicco-bar Islands	1.75	2.53	0.92
2.	Arunachal Pradesh	7.21	6.14	8.33
3.	Chandigarh	1.32	2.00	0.54
4.	Dadra & Nagar Haveli	8.21	7.33	9.12
5.	Delhi	1.16	1.87	0.37
6.	Goa, Daman & Diu	2.45	2.07	2.85
7.	Lakshadweep	0.34	0.36	0.31
8.	Mizoram	3.23	2.94	3.53
9.	Pondicherry	1.63	2.11	1.51

Note : 1. *Based on 5% advance tabulation of 1981 Census.

2. Figures for rest of the states and all Union Territories are based on 100% processing of 1981 Census data.

3. 1981 Census figures for Andhra Pradesh, Orissa and Tamil-Nadu are not available. 1981 Census not not conducted in Assam. According to the 1971 Census, the percentage of workers in these states are as follows :

Aadhra Pradesh	9.24	11.81	6.62
Assam	3.41	6.04	0.74
Orissa	5.30	9.07	1.49
Tamil Nadu	4.58	6.22	2.82

Since great attention is being paid to children now (1979 being the International year of the child) the 1981 census has taken into account the various fields where children of both sexes are being employed. The 1981 census have classified 9 groups of works mainly, viz.

1981 Census of Indian Child Labourers[12]

	No. of child workers between the age of 0-14 years in thousands	*Percentage*
Agricultural labourers	4,774	42.76
Construction	79	0.72
Transport, storage, etc.	34	0.29
Cultivation	4,013	35.95
Livestock	704	6.30
Mining and quarrying	27	0.23
Manufacturing processing, etc	1,930	13.14
Trade Commerce	246	2.20
Other services	326	2.92
Total	11,168	100%

Strangely enough, organized and unorganized begging finds no place in the list of children's occupation. A great social worker Mrs. Padmini Sen Gupta once observed : "Begging is becoming a real profession and there are scaring rumours that gangsters and syndicates of human beings trade in human babies and children. Certainly the mother clad in a rag and clutching a baby in her arms is a sight that is shameful... children are drugged or even one hears tortured. To see pavement dwellers in all their horrors living in filth, children picking up rejected and popping food mixed with filth into their mouths makes one feel desperate...there should be proper deterrant action...."[13]

12. The Hindustan Times, Patna Nov. 15, 1988.
13. Sen Gupta, Padmini, "Child Labour as a Social Problem", (contributed article) refer p. 7 of *Child Labour in Indla*, op. cit.

Apart from begging which is debatable if it is a profession, there is the unrecorded case of child as a bonded labour especially in villages. Parents obtain loan and put their child as security who is a real mortgage until freed which is rare.

It is therefore imperative that we study the areas of child labour in India's context so that we can fully appreciate the dimensions of our own problem : 'Child Labour in Bhagalpur Silk Industry'.

The incidence of child labour is the highest in Andhra Pradesh and lowest in Kerala. It makes 9% of the total labour force, 9.2% of total child population and 3.7% of the total population of the state. In fact, Andhra Pradesh accounts for 15.2 per cent of the total child workers in the country. Kerala gave out a paradoxical situation. Because of the states high wage economy, many of the traditional industries of the state were shifting to neighbouring states. Cashew nut processing and coir industries are native to Kerala, but they cannot accommodate much labour. Literacy is very high, as such children of Kerala cannot be induced to work under inhuman conditions.

Normally, more children are working in the unorganized agricultural sector. Child labour force is being controlled in factories, as such there is a steep decline in their numbers. But there is upsurge in the mushroom growth of unregulated factories and workshops where the number of children being employed is increasing by leaps and bounds. These are largely Small Scale Industries, spreading their tentacles in the four corners of our country. A large number of children are employed in Bidi manufacture centres in Madhya Pradesh, Maharashtra, Tamil Nadu, West Bengal and even Bihar. 'The unsponsored recruit system come handy to run away boys who leave their families, remain anonymous in cities after snapping their moorings in villages and even the family, taking whatever job comes their way and thus remain exposed to be risks of urban life.[14]

Children in cities perform a much larger variety of jobs than in villages because urban economics present an extensively diversified structure. In agriculture that is in rural areas, all jobs centre round crop-raising. Ploughing, sowing, transplantation, weeding, harvesting, and other unclassified works keep children enjoined with their family, where their labour is not accounted for against their wages, nor are their mother's or father's. But urban jobs are wage oriented. The 1961 census reports :

"Out of the 77 thousand male child migrant workers in the cities of India, 90 per cent were occupied in three occupational divisions namely crafts men and labourers (43.5%), services (36.9%), and sales (10.9%). Nearly 60% of them were employed in five occupational divisions namely : (i) housekeeper, cooks, maids etc. (24.8%), (ii) labourers not elsewhere classified (10.7%), (iii) waiters, bartenders etc. (7.3%), (iv) salesmen, shop assistants etc. (7.1%), (v) spinners, weavers, knitters, dyers etc. (6.5%). Out of the 21 thousand migrant working jobs, 90% were employed in the two occupational divisions : (i) Services (44.9%), (ii) craftmen and labourers (44.1%). About two thirds of the working girls were employed in three occupational categories : (i) housekeepers, cooks, maids etc. (40.6%), (ii) labourers not elsewhere classified (14.6%), and (iii) spinners, weavers, knitters, dyers etc (11.3%).[15]

Considering the job situations for children in cities, we find in Bombay, urchins employed in production units, trade

14. Cf. 'Working Children in Urban Delhi' op. cit., p. 29.

15. Report of the Committee on Child Labour, op. cit., p 15 Taken from Sebastian A., 'Statiwise Child Migrants and Child Migrant Labour in the Cities of India'. A paper presented in New Delhi, March, 1979.

and commerce, arts & crafts, service and repairs, construction works, domestic service, hotel/restaurant, casual labour, scrap colllection. Boys and girls both enter into such jobs : boys earn three times more than girls. In Madras, similar job opportunities appear before them. Shivakasi in Tamil Nadu offers them works in matches and fire works industry. Tamil Nadu prospers with children in bidi industry. Likewise in Murshidabad, in Bengal, where Biri, muslin and silk go together. Firozabad is the home town of Bangles industry. Children perform Jurai (joinning) Chhatai (Sorting), Katai (engraving and cutting designs), Pakai (heating glass), finally Ginai (counting) and packing for despatch. Bhadohi and Mirzapur in the United Provinnces are famous for carpet weaving, where children are carried preposterously and forcibly ushered into the job. In recent times plenty of such criminal acts have been discovered and reported viz., kidnapping and stealing children between 6-14 years of age. In Calcutta (West Bengal) children are a common sight in machine tools and repair shops apart from being rag tag boys or little errand men. In tool and repair shops, we see these future of the nation blundering into ashes and poisonous fumes.

Children are deft in stone polishing, gold polish, Meena making in Rajasthan. Sometimes they outwit the adults due to their nimble fingers. The young diamond cutters of Surat develop eye trouble too soon, but there they are unmindful of their own future. But at Kanchipuram (Tamil Nadu), and in Bangalore (Karnataka), children are better off in silk industry, perfumes and Agarbatti manufacture.

These set the stage for examining children's participation in the silk industry of Bhagalpur. Decidedly state governments' attention has been scant on this issue resulting in the flourishing of child labour in the silk industry of Bhagalpur. We meet two types of children in the field—one, the weaver's own child, male and female both, and two, the children coming from villages as hired labour. Here too they form an accountable force in silk industry ; they are the corner stone of silk manufacture. Again, as elsewhere, so here too, they are the lowest paid staff, and in some cases they are bonded labour, on whose person or mortgage, his parents have received money on incredible interest.

The child's participation begins from dyeing. The dyer boils the skeins in soap and water, a process which removes the natural gum and leaves them soft and lusturous. They are then rinsed and passed on the dye vat. Then the child puts these yarns on bamboo hangers for drying. It is then taken for dipping into cooked rice gruel (starch) and is called applying 'Mari' (माड़ी). This gives the yarn toughness and straightens them. The yarns are again put in the Sun to dry. Now begins the process of reeling the yarns in bobbins where they are put to sizing. The grown up child touching 14 years of age commonly put the prepared yarns on beams. In Bhagalpur silk industry technically this is called Bai (बय) Bharai after which the yarns are passed one by one into reeds. Now when the yarns are ready, they are placed on the looms whether it is handloom or powerloom. The threads running lengthwise are called the warp and those running crosswise to bind the warp to make the fabric are called the weft or filling or 'shot' or picks'. In local language these are called Tani/Bharni. The process of putting the threads on the beam to be placed in the loom is commoly called as warping. Before the final stage the child sits with a spinning wheel (made from bamboo sticks) and fulfils the task of Nari Bharai. The older craftsmen now sit at the shuttle and weave pleasant patterns of silk fabric.

Waste threads are bound to come out as weaving goes on. Here again the child labour is called in to collect them and pile them in different sizes, colour and class of threads. While the manufactured cloth or silk is once again straightened, flattened and smoothened before it is taken to the market, the child lends his helping hand in the entire process. These are taken to traders and exporters who do the calendering and final polishing after treatment in chemical mixed water. The waste threads are taken to small traders who turn them into strong threads used for rituals like Raksha Bandhan and Anant (रक्षाबंधन और अनंत), and threads or laces for amulets and lockets and armlets etc.

The child labour in the silk industry of Bhagalpur therefore performs not less than fourteen items of work[16] that preface the final manufacture of silk cloth. He lives through hazards of health but quite unmindful of what happens to him tomorrow. He lives bereft of education and enlightenment except what cinema films fill into his mind, heart and soul. He lives for today, struggling and seeking a pittance for his existence. Since he lives in dark about the national progressive movements he lives without clamour, fully at peace with his parents, guardians and employers cherishing a dream of a prosperous tomorrow.

To sum up therefore, we have considered the difference between voluntary participation of children in silk industry of Bhagalpur, purposeful vocational training and child's wage earning and consequent exploitation of child labour. We have also dealt with the factors that contribute to this inhuman practice of snatching away light and life from pretty but poor children of the soil for self-gain. Even forty years after the achievement of independence we live in the days of Charles Dickens and those American Novelists who exposed cruelty to children through forced labour. Silk industry of Bhagalpur is not without this slur which needs a humanising touch. King Midus exists in every heart—more prominently in those who

16. These fourteen works are locally called :
सूत रंगाई, सुखाई, माड़ी दिलाई, सुखायी, बोबिन भराई, साइज करायी, बीम मोड़ाई, वय भराई, रीढ चढ़ाई, मशीन लोड, नरी भराई, सूत मिलाई, साइज बनाई, आदि आदि ।

cannot bridle their lust for golden touch. Child labour stands as an antithesis to modern humanism and cultured pride. Deeper investigation into the proportion of child labour engaged in silk industry of Bhagalpur and the magnitude of their exploitation shall be probed in the chapters that follow.

CHAPTER IV

Review of Literature

There is paucity of literature on children in India, there is marked scarsity of literature on child labour in India, and practically there is no work no child labour in the Silk Industry of Bhagalpur. Informative texts on child labour employed in different trades are few and far between. Prior to India's independence from British rule, child labour was no concern of the administrator, researcher or the litterateure. England and America had, of course produced large number of novels, novellettes and poems describing the agonies of children working in and around chimneys, but India was more or less mum on the topic. Albert Cames had in his famous work, 'L' Homme Revolte' drawn the attention of the world through his epigrammatic statement. "If we cannot make a world in which children no longer suffer, at least we can try to reduce the number of suffering children", and this cry did not go in vain. Earlier, Charles Dickens had raised his voice against social injustice meted out to poor children. No novelist before Dickens had treated the lower middle classes on such broad lines or in so frank a way".[1] He had created an 'immediate

1. Legouis & Cazamian, *A History of English Literature*, London, 1951, p. 1130.

community' or 'instinctive fraternity' with those quivering images of anguish and soul debasing poverty and the result was a David Copperfield, Great Expectations or Oliver Twist. In America likewise, Mark Twain gave to the world, horrendous figures of masters and the timid lamb-like children working in sun and rain under cruel lashes, in Tom Sawyer, Huckleberry Finn & others. If Dickens observed, felt and created characters as antithesis of the promises of Industrial Revolution and monopolistic opulence, Mark Twain saw the cruel and ignonimous features of Negro Slave Trade rampant in America. Dickens's workhouse chapters remain singularly impressive. Mark Twain's children, fugitive, hungry and bonded are 'economic' boys and economic issues of American life that were preposterous during the settlement days.

In Indian literatures children are extolled, admired and loved, but there is no Balkand for suffering children so far. Children make universal brotherhood possible, they make a world community of loving objects from their birth. Jealousy and dissension enter our hearts as we grow : mental and physical frontiers appear as our bones stiffen. Yet none can deny, "children are our future, they are the seed for the hoped for harvest of the world—as precious and as rich in promise as the carefully-nurtured wheat grains of the knowing farmer."[2] Indian literary creativity on this aspect is still awaited.

But one spectacle is grim and ugly. Children are the chosen servants, working hands, in homes and looms, farms, chimneys, tailors, shoemakers, errand boys in banks and roadside stalls—say, everywhere. Their condition deserves indepth study, spherewise, zonewise etc. Mention has been made sparsely about child labour in Encyclopaedias (Even Moses was a child slave in Egypt) but they are slowly drawing greater

2. From the speeches of Maurice Pate (1894-1965), UNICEF's first Executive Director.

attention in various fora, research papers, reports, journals etc. The Indian Labour Organivation report, or the Reports of Statistical Departments, both of the Centre and the States, are not enough, far less satisfactory. Reports collected under the aegis of the UNICEF and WHO are really impressive. Census reports and reports contained in Sociological abstracts are good pointers to the fact that much remains to be done to enlighten public about sordid neglect of our children. As such, some books and periodicals are coming out to fulfil the task, but the loudest voice is being raised by journals and daily newspapers, and seminar discussions of stupendous strength and magnificent values. We will therefore begin with a review of available literatures from published books, first.

What meets our eye immediately is a valuable book 'Child Labour in the Meaning of the Times and other Speeches' by A.J. Beveridge, published in 1908. The author has made an impassioned appeal to save children from losing their physical health and mental growth by undergoing painful existence in jobs. If his normal development is interfered with, then his chances for a normal life is destroyed. Its purpose is to awaken people to the unworthy inhuman practice to employ child in hard labour.

'The International Handbook of Child Care and Protection', published from London in 1928 by E. Fuller contains ample references to incongruities in society that lead to child labour. It has an appeal to desist from the cruel practice of utilising children in manufacturing concerns.

K.D. Lumpkin, and D.W. Douglas published a book 'Child Workers in America' (1937) which has been followed by a rich crop of literature on the subject. Correct portrayal of the child workers in the different federating states of U.S.A. make the subject matter of these literatures interesting. At least they succeed in creating an awarness of the social imbalance in a democratic set-up. Grace Abbott's illuminating work 'The Child and State' in two volumes issued from the University of

Chicago Press in 1938 is a land Mark in itself. The work of Frank. J. Gohen entitled 'Children in Trouble' published by W.W. Norton & Co., New York in 1952 falls in this group of literature of awakening. 'The Child Wants a Home, Foster Home', How and why ? prepared by Isobel Mordy George and printed by G. Harraps & Co. Ltd., London is a still more vigorous call for sympathetic treatment to the unfortunate bread earners, that is, the child. In the same category falls the book 'The Child and His Welfare' written by Hazal Frederickson, and published by W.H. Freeman & Co., San Fransisco, California.

But England and America took cognisance not only of the social aspect of child labour, but also of the legal necessity of removing disabilities that the working child was facing everyday. Balshevik Russia had no such problem to tackle since socialism in action kept the child safe in his home and school. But economic inequality and poverty are a widespread phenomenon of capitalist system where childhood of the born unfortunate is victimised unsparingly. But a civilised society cannot allow such situation to pass unnoticed. The government has to take executive as well as legislative steps to undo the social evil. Law is a turning wheel because society is always on the move. Consequently, much renewal and amendments take place in laws to keep pace with the social dynamism. The protection of the child against exploitation is more desirable, hence a debate on the issues goes on endlessly. The International Labour Organisation is wide awake to the problem of the unlucky urchins. Once again, it has to be mentioned that England & America are still discovering lacunae in their national laws protecting the child, and they are tirelessly forging out national schemes to give to their children congenial atmosphere to grow into a full man.

For this purpose the Children's Bureau, Department of Labour, United States, made an enquiry 'Why Child Labour Laws', in 1946, followed by a work by Jeremy P. Felt "Hostage of fortune : Child Labour Reforms in the New York State', which was published at Syracuse University Press in 1965. A little earlier in 1923, R.G. Fuller had prepared a treatise 'Child Labour and the Constitution' which was published from New York. 'Constitutional Politics in the Progressive Era—Child Labour and the Law', saw the light of the day in 1968 from the University of Chicago Press, prepared by S.B. Wood. The Ontario Department of Public Welfare, Toronto, Canada, brought out a valuable brochure 'The Child Welfare Act and Regulation' which highlighted the importance of legal protection of the child. Such necessity was felt due to zonal studies of children's condition which were compiled, e.g. in 'Child Care Standards in Ohio, Published by Ohio State Department of Public Welfare, U.S.A. and in 'Labour's Untold Story', written by R.O. Boyer & M.M. Herbert and published from New York in 1955. A. Bimba too had not forgotten to include child labour in his compendium, "History of the Working American Class' published in 1927 from New York, U.S.A.

In fact war leaves a legacy of destitutes and orphans. The First World War had thrown on the streets millions of unattended children who were destined to die due to social inability to care for them. The spectacle caught the attention of Eglantyne Jebb who produced a five clause charter for children which was an urgent saving device. This charter came to be called the Declaration of Geneva. The League of Nations in its plenary session dated 26th September 1924, unanimously adopted the Declaration of Geneva and the member states accepted to be guided by its principles. But before the measures could reach the children, another war broke out only after fifteen years and before the Second World War came to a close, millions and millions of children, waifs, maimed, neglected, God's little lambs lay dying without an epitaph.

But cruelty and sympathy reside as eternal tenants in human hearts. The Second World War brought to light the futility of such massive military exercises. Instead, come home to every nation the idea that fraternity was a better substitute for fratricide. The United Nations Organization was born out of this realisation, with two convictions. One—geographical separation is no guarantee of peace, and two—collective security is the only means of survival. Naturally, the U.N.O. took a vow to "save succeeding generations from the scourge of war by achieving international cooperation in solving international problem of an economic, social, cultural or humon character, and for promoting and encouraging respect for human rights and for fundamental freedoms for all without distinction as to race, sex language or religion".[3] The U.N.O. therefore became an association of sovereign states engaged harmoniously in achieving enduring peace. This international forum became "a town meeting of the world" where the fragrance of amity and tolerance hung in the soothing air. The General Assembly of the United Nations created 'Specialized Agencies' like Internotional Labour Office, Food and Agriculture Organization, International Monetary Fund, International Bank of Reconstruction and Development, United Nations Educational, Scientific, and Cultural Organization (UNESCO), World Health Organization (WHO) and bore the mantle of World trusteeship on itself.

The United Nations Organization could not overlook or bypass the pressing problem of the children of the world. In 1959, the United Nations General Assembly adopted a ten point Declaration of the Rights of the child. Death and disease in the aftermath of the War in the four corners of the globe demanded a new universal approach to the child's claim for survival. It was for the first time in human history that such a consideration was on the anvil. The United Nations action for refugees and distressed people or homeless children was established during the World War II years from 1946, as the United Nations International Children's Emergency Fund.

3. Gettell, Raymond Garfield. "Modern Political Thought", World Press, Calcutta, 1950, p. 485.

To begin with UNICEF's major purpose was to give relief to children who are victims of war and to promote better health and nutrition. But in subsequent years enormous changes have taken place in its operation in all member countries of the U.N.O...' UNICEF's theme was "His name is Today'.[4] His needs are immediate. A child's claim on society cannot be delayed or postponed lest there is no tomorrow for him.

The United Nations General Assembly in their unanimous resolution of 1959 undertaking to fulfil the Declaration of Rights of the Child agreed to :

(1) Give a name and nationality, and equal status to every child at birth.

(2) Maternal protection and family care.

(3) Health care and protection against diseases.

(4) Adequate nutrition and adequate shelter.

(5) Education.

(6) Play and recreation.

(7) Social protection irrespective of colour, race, language etc.

(8) Protection from work for the child, and for exploitation for youth.

(9) Special care for physically, mentally or socially handicapped children such as orphans, retarded children etc.

(10) Protection from racial, religious and other form of discrimination.[5]

A child was the real beneficiary now. The developed countries, politically called the major powers, had shown the way to the developing and underdeveloped countries. The light beamed by the UNO General Assembly pierced Indian horizon

4. Baig, Tara Ali, "Our Children", Govt. of India, New Delhi, Dec. 1979, p. 49-50.
5. de Souza, Alfred, "Children in India", New Delhi, 1979, p. 4.

also. Contribution by the international agencies towards child welfare was remarkable in India too. "The UNICEF has given and is still maintaining its flow of assistance to rural primary health centres, nutrition programmes, family and child welfare schemes, pre-vocational training, Integrated Child Development Services Projects, Applied Nutrition Programme in rural areas, science education and a variety of other programmes in India. World Health Organization (W.H.O.) has assisted India in developing child health services as integral part of maternity and child welfare and nutritional services. Likewise, the UNESCO and the ILO have also helped in child education and prevention of child labour respectively. The International Union for Child Welfare, CARE and other International voluntary agencies have taken keen interest in development of child welfare in India".[6] Consequently, a national policy for child welfare has been framed from 1974. The Indian Parliament approved country's first Child Welfare Policy Statement (in 1974) which stated that the children are a nation's supremely important asset and that their programmes must find a prominent place in our national plans for the development of human resources. In 1974 itself, the Indian Council for Child Welfare had submitted an 8 point policy statement to government emphasising two points especially, viz, that investment in the child represented investment in the human capital of our Five Year Plans, and the second—that the unwanted child should not be born. There should be family limitation so that dignified living for each child can be secured. The National Children's Board is working directly under the Prime Minister in the company of Senior Central Ministers.[7]

6. Choudhary, D. Paul, "Child Welfare/Development" New Delhi, 1980. p. 16.
7. The ICCW's national plan for children clearly reflects the influence of UNICEF mandate discussed earlier. The U.N.O.'s Generai Assembly has been evolving ways and means tirelessly to the theme of 'Today's Children—Tomorrow's World'. The UNICEF was created in 1946. In December 1950 the General

(Contd.)

This rather elaborate discussion of the U.N.O., UNICEF, & UNESCO and allied agencies, has been unavoidable because their findings and directive have gone a long way to mould the Government of India's policies towards children's welfare. Even other developing and underdeveloped countries are following the same route to reach the target of building up child's future. Plenty of literature has now been produced with the awareness floodgates of which have been opened by the UNICEF and such related agencies. The realisation is acute that the neglect of the child breeds a social crisis, and if it is allowed to deepen, then political criris is not far off. New dimensions shall then be added to the latter leading to an upsurge in national and international instability which is another name for violence, environmental deterioration and social rumpus. Luckily a feeling has dawned among social workers and litterateures that at present many millions of children are growing up in circumstances which are deleterious to their growth, and this has become a self-perpetuating cycle leaving the seeds of its own renewal. Eminent thinkers have come to the conclusion that a child is at the centre of political and economic concern. In the bringing up of our children are sown the seeds of peace and prosperity or of violence and degradation. Therefore the Indian National Policy for children laid down[8] that "a child is an investment in the future of the

Assembly reformed the UNICEF mandate to respond to the silent yet desperate needs of countless numbers of children in developing countries. UNICEF became a permanent arm of the United Nation's System. Gradually, the UNICEF began to reach out to underdeveloped countries calling them to adopt protective nutrition, health care and basic education measures for the mother and the child. Thus has began a global partnership for children and an intense consciousness about children's plight with the declaration of the year 1979 as International Year of the Child.

8. Indian National Policy for children are enumerated as eight which are given below :

(1) Quoted above. *(Contd.)*

nation and must therefore, be an integral part of economic planning". Obviously, therefore our books, journals, seminars and our entire consensus of opinion derive their energy and sustenance from these pronouncements which we will witness hereafter in our review of literature concerning child labour and child welfare.

Decidedly the impulse released by UNICEF compelled people to investigate and report on the condition of the rising generation. Dorothy Zietz's Child's Welfare, Principles and Method published in 1959 from New York, was in consequence of the consciousness unleashed by UNICFF. Yet, it was a subjective treatment and carried not much of objective study. But the shortcoming was filling up by a specialised publication of the UNICEF entitled—'Children of the Developing

(2) Education must have a primary objective the creation of a whole human being. For a country still 80% agricultural, educational orientation is imperative to achieve a national goal of production and self-sufficency.

(3) A child, like all growing things, must be assured specific essentials (like preventive health, nutrition etc.) at each stage of its growth and development to adulthood.

(4) A child must be a partner in normal family life, with access to family, skills, crafts and responsibilities.

(5) A nationwide sanitation programme in which the child can participate, learn and teach new habits of cleanliness is essential to reduce high mortality for children from intestinal, fly borne and water-borne diseases.

(6) The child should grow with dignity, self reliance and a sense of responsibility towards others.

(7) All programmes, mass media, school curricula, etc. must contain definitive policies to unite diversity and remove prejudices in the minds of children.

(8) Legislation must establish the objectives of the U.N. Declaration of the Right of the Child signed by India in 1959.

(Taken from Tara Ali Baig's book "Our Children" *op. cit.* p. 334-335).

Countries, in 1963'. Bihar took a cue from these efforts and 'An Annual Report on the working of the Employment of Children (Act 1938); for the year 1963 was published in 1965 by the Bihar Government's Labour Departement (Factory), Ranchi. Some writers made detours and prepared educative treatises like 'Children Development and Relationships' as for example by Mollie S. Sonar in 1967. There were others who strove to unfold the conditions of labouring children and made investigative reports as in a book 'Children Under Stress' published by the Penguin Press, London, and prepared by Sula, Wolf in 1970.

"Child Labour in India" was the result of an academic pursuit of Jinesh Chandra Kulshrestha (1978) and projected a vision of jurists, legislators, social thinkers, economists and philanthropists. The main focus is on the legal aspect of child labour which has been composed in seven chapters. Child labour and its social implications, causes of child labour e.g. poverty, large family, illiteracy, child labour as a cheap commodity, are indeed quite cogent discussions. Tradition of child labour in different countries viz, America, England and Soviet Russia and in India have been briefly but wisely discussed. Soviet Russia indeed has restricted employment of children in hazardous works by legislation and by arousing social conscience. A National Code of Labour is in vogue in Russia right from 1932 and it prohibits night and overtime labour by children. Children below 15 years can be taken only for education work. Medical check up is essential. Maximum permitted hours of work is 6 hours. Summer holidays are provided to working lads and lasses also. These could fruitfully be adopted by India as well.

Due to the role of the International Labour Organization towards child labour, constitutional provision in Indian laws with more schemes and more protective measures have been attempted. These references make it a fine compendium of

Labour laws for working children and much of the matter is useful for Indian researchers.

The International Year of the Child (1979) saw a great harvest of useful literature on children, quite a lot concerned with working children. Lela B. Costin's book 'Child Welfare : Policies and Practice, (Published 1979) draws attention to the fact that any movement for social uplift is incomplete without adeqaute concern for child welfare. Rightly, the child is the future adult citizen and so the society must translate this conviction into action. Not only the well-being, rather preparing the child for availing himself of full opportunities of life must be guaranteed to him. In a way, and of course a forceful way Lela B. Costin has defined the goal of child welfare which every nation must pursue and attain.

The Indian Council for Child Welfare was also sponsoring informative and educative literature. The Department of Social Welfare in the Ministry of Education and Social Welfare funded such projects and also publication of their findings. A good report was produced on "Working Children in Urban Delhi" (A study of their life and work) in 1977 which revealed many facets of the child labour force. Though the report centred round the nature of the work performed by children and their number involved, yet the project wandered in many spheres, as for example, the Municipal Licensing system covering those establishments where young hands are employed, the socio-economic parameters in order to detect the working and living conditions of workers, character of occupation, the occupational nexus in the home i.e. between the parents and the child, wages and earnings, method of recruitment, influence of caste and religion and such related topics. The project is studied in the end in the background of the labour laws of the land. In fact this makes the book a handy guide for further research in other cities and other environs.

Alfred de Souza made a landmark by editing a book

'Children in India, in 1979'. The book is the result of a generous collaboration of eminent scholars and practitioners. It is hoped that their ideas, experience and concern for under privileged children in India will stimulate reflection on policy and action to ensure the human development of millions of children during the International Year of the Child and the decade that follows. The contributions have been classified under such heads as 'Critical Perspectives on the Under Developed Child' whether he/she belongs to the rural or the urban area. 'Child Health Care, Health Knowledge, Nutrition', which includes an essay on the training of the health auxiliaries for basic health service. Aspects of socialisation : Alternative Forms of Child Care', which has a very useful chapter on 'The Neglected Child and the Law'. The book has succeeded in putting the child in the limelight, as well as his needs and problems. It has constructive suggestions, some poignant indications of what we actually need to do to benefit children. Even budgetary commitments are hinted at in this compilation.

What is remarkable about the book is the emphasis on the cooperation of non-government agencies in order to strengthen governmental measures issued for ameliorating child's plight, and for that purpose attempting at social awakening. True, incredible amount of activity, and real interest have begun for the coming generations' welfare. An infrastructure of legal and social policy has been delineated simulataneously for child's protection against hazardous employment and obvious exploitation. Indeed, law and help from non-government sector can help the processes of policy development and balanced planning.

The book, published on the 20th anniversary of the U.N. Declaration of the Rights of the Child (in 1959) is a reiteration of the "cooperation of the community of nations in the common task of meeting the basic needs of children nutrition, health, education, maternal protection and family care, equal social status and protection from racial and other forms of discrimination.[9] In short it is a reassertion of the child's right to live with dignity, even though he may be poor, illiterate or otherwise depressed in the society. His social value, his rights and obligations are the same that go with the rich boy, prosperous and high in the community. The book rightly, concludes on a note of cooperation : "The Government of India also calls upon the citizens, State Governments, local bodies, educational institutions and voluntary organizations to play their part in the overall effort to attain these objectives".[10]

In dealing with Smt. Tara Ali Baig we are dealing with a colossus, and her book 'Our Children' (1979), a *magnum opus* By the time the book came to see the light of the day, she had accomplished a twenty-three year involvement in child welfare planning and organization both in India and abroad. She was the President of the International Union for Child Welfare in 1977, which was founded in 1919, and had prepared the first charter for children in 1924 which later became the basis for the U.N. Declaration of the Rights of the Child in 1959.

It was the vision of Smt. Baig that 'programmes for children should be an integral part of economic and social development plans' because 'the problem of the child is no less and no more than that of the society's own future. Smt. Baig provides us with an abundance of insight into the problems of the child which she deals most exhaustively. Her canvas is larger than other writers on Indian children for she had a conviction that the mother occupies a central position in the Indian family. Attention inevitably turns to the status and role of women within the family leading to a rather striking observation that "the sense of maternal duty and devotion is probably the sheet anchor of the Indian Child". This proposition adds a new dimension to the study of the problems surrounding Indian boys and girls which most of the writers pass over with dis-

9. de Souza, Alfred, "Children in India" Delhi, 1979, p. XV.
10. Ibid., p. 253 App. II.

asterous consequence. Smt. Baig rightly asserts that high fertility and high mortality of the mother and the child go together for these are tragically coupled with indifferent and inadequate mother and child care.

The thrust of Smt. Baig's argument is, therefore, at following up an adequate concretization of perspectives that should guide the effective incorporation of that, or any revised and upgraded, plan of action for child development. The author discusses three broad aspects of the problem, namely, the cultural milieu, the demographic position and the specifics of the evolution of child welfare movement, and then proceeds to discuss in depth the major issues in child development related to work and employment, education, health and nutrition, special position of the child in the tribal setting, entertainment and leisure time activity, the physical and social handicaps, legislation for social defence, training resources ; needs and methodologies, government's role both at the policy making and administrative levels, and the role of voluntary efforts. The exposition of each of these issues deals with historical trends, the present position and the likely future course of development. Smt. Baig's exposition is free, frank, unsparing and adequately self searching, bold and relevant to the extreme. She does not categorize children by subjects as the pre-school child etc. Instead she asserts, "it is not a butterfly on a pin to be examined and put into separate trays but a living breathing sentient being whose needs in any category whatsoever are simply love, security, food, liberation from disease and education for growth in their own environment". She has also pleaded for the usual logic placed for child's engagement in productive work, e.g. in rural sphere. "Work by the child, especially within the family, is not necessarily counter-productive for the child's own development in the prevailing social and economic conditions in rural areas where the bulk of our population lives. It is maintained, for example that "a child who works from early infancy generally has some important discipline' and that 'a child who contributes to his family resources is the child who belongs'. In fact, this phenomenon is in evidence among the families of Weavers of Silk at Bhagalpur where their own children and neighbour's and villager's children show their skill, training and capacity to earn their bread.

Smt. Tara Ali Baig maintains a holistic approach towards the problem of the child. In the introduction to her book Sri P.B. Desai maintains that Smt. Baig rightly deplores that "no-clear-cut attitude has yet emerged to meet our special problem of one of the largest dependent population in the world and to integrate it with overall development". She peristently pleads that "the item of expenditure upon children and youth must be considered by policy makers as of equal importance to investment in other fields". Even though man's conscience has expanded and is growing liberal gradually by dropping the idea of children as totally dependents and also personal possessions, yet a family awareness has to dawn that ability and natural incentive must grow in children so that they be masters of their own lot in rapidly approaching time.

Side by side, the case of the special child, the physically and socially handicapped child, the blind, deaf, dumb, polio-striken and paralysed child deserves compassionate attention of the government and the society. Smt. Baig's book is therefore quite comprehensive and fully supported by relevant statistics.

A prolific writer Dr. D. Paul Chowdhary has been actively connected with the Central Social Welfare Board, Indian Council for Child Welfare, National Institute of Public Cooperation and Child Development and the Department of Rural Development. While working with these departments he felt the necessity of a manual on child welfare development for the guidance of workers in this field. In fact it was a long felt gap and the professional social worker and home scientists could hardly make a headway without it. As such the author prepared a volume 'Child Welfare and Development' which was published in 1980. The volume begins with a discussion on the historical development of child welfare and briefly covers the scope of child welfare development services like creche, balwadi, Bal Bhavan etc. The case of the handicapped children, the mentally retarded ones, has also been adequately dealt with.

Dr. Chowdhry's book has come out at the appropriate time when the International Year of the Child was still being celebrated. The book has surveyed other Indian products on the subject and it is right to say that the author has combined his personal experience with those of international workers and prepared a good reference book as this present volume.

He has started categorywise e.g. Child Health, Pre-School Child, Child Recreation, Destitute Child, Problems of Services and Programmes for and by the Youth, Handicapped Children, Prevention and Treatment of Juvenile Delinquency, along with general topics, appendices on legal measures etc. There is a rich collection of statistical material in his book which are thought provoking. He informs that "there are 11 million working children in India which constitute 5 to 10 per cent of child population, of which 8 million are boys and 3 million are girls. Around 93% of working children belong to the rural areas which is around 6% of the child population. 108 million children live in varying degree of destitution, 91% in villages and 17% in the towns. Around 2.5% belong to the Schedule Castes and Schedule Tribes. There are 1.5 lakhs begging and vagrant children, 4.2 million children belong to migrant families. Around 50 million children live in conditions averse to survival. 126 million children may be living below poverty line".[11] Such is the demographic profile speaking through a grim and dark statistics.

11. Chowdhary, D. Paul, "Child Welfare/Development" Delhi, 1980, p. 416.

These figures naturally lead us to collect news from local studies which point us to the fact that immediate action is imperative.

'Child Labour in Patna' (1979) is a zonal study by Alakh Narayan Sharma. He too impinges his arguments based on statistics called from UNESCO's Statistical Year Book, 1976. He gloomily mentions that India's per capita expenditure on child education was the lowest at 30 paise per child in 1976. In India 42% of the population is under the age of 14, whereas in U.S.A, or Sweden the dependent population is only 22%. Children mortality rate is also very high in India, particularly due to malnutrition. Sunken eyes and bloated bellies are the pictures not only of African or Ethiopean boys, rather the same picture obtains in Indian villages also.

Sri Sharma rightly points out that the high number of young lads working at Patna are a result of high birth rate in their families, high rural emigration, and low economic capacity.

While the accurate number of floating establishments in Patna has not been arrived at, yet it may safely be conjectured at a few thousand, distributed among Bidi, Shellac, Mica, Cloth, Printing, Carpet weaving, fire works, soap and candle making, cloth weaving & tea-stall or automobile repair/servicing centres.

Leela Gulati has likewise taken to review 'Child Labour in Kerala's Coir Industry' and her study is restricted to a few selected villages in Kerala. The review was done in 1980. She has offered some significant information about Coir Cottage industry which is as widespread as the silk industry in Bhagalpur. There is similarity in children's engagement in both the industries, with the difference that boys and girls in Kerala attend to their employment, as well as, attend their schools. At Bhagalpur, the boys and girls spend all their time with weaving and ancilliary duties, giving a complete go by to schools. Mrs. Gulati observes that drop outs from schools in Kerala are minimal wherein girls take more to schooling in addition to the household industry. In Kerala the occupational status of employed children is high because their parents also carry on the job. In Bhagalpur silk industry the position is reverse : Occupational children are backward in everything except in mimicking cinema episodes. There is, however, one more similarity between Kerala coir industry and Bhagalpur silk industry. It is in the area of workers. Both Hindus (Tantis) and Muslim (Julaha or Momins) equally partake of the fruits of silk industry and are proud artisans of their trade.

These regional studies have induced people to invade the private reserves of several types of industries which employ children under a profiteering urge. Piecemeal rate is historically a method for capitalists' boundless profit and it has a control device also. As opposed to this is time rate system which is often spurned by employers, as the piecemeal system is more paying. Such a situation of utter exploitation is witnessed in the match and firework industry of Shivkasl in Saltur Taluka, Tamil Nadu. Poverty of a family is the main reason for parents to send their children to Shivkasi's numberless factories where it is all hazard. As such, Shivkasi has come to publie view in recent times, and opinions do not favour children's participation in such an undertaking where sulphur and phosphorus and such chemicals are used. The Madras Institute of Development Studies have published much adverse report on Shivkasi in 1985. Similarly the welfare agencies in Uttar Pradesh have spoken bitterly about the state of affairs in Bhadohi and Mirzapur carpet factories.

A compilation entitled 'Working Children in Bombay A Study', published by the National Institute of Public Cooperation and Child Development, New Delhi, repeats the same findings as poverty of a family inciting child labour. Fifty two percent of the families surveyed by the agency reported a meagre earning of Rs. 25/- to Rs. 500/- a month to which children contributed 23% of the family income. About 47.4% of the families were running in debts. Child labour was a subsidy therefore but the young kids were facing full 8 hours to 14 hours of working each day.

Pitiable though the condition of the child is in every manufacturing concern or in unorganized sectors, this report makes its presence felt due to a strong anti-thesis view. The study is against any measures meant to abolish child labour. It asserts : "As long as the level of our economic development is what it is, any thought of abolishing child labour would be an unrealistic and undesirable proposition, a pious intent without a relevance to contemporary social pragmatics. In the absence of possible alternatives, a rash abolitionist measure would simply aggravate the misery of the poor".[12] In short, the abolition of child labour would mean the extinction of the child's family.

'A study done on child labour of another metropolitan city, Ahmedabad,[13] also found that acute poverty was responsible for forcing the young children in labour brigade. Poverty and illiteracy went together to push the children to hell. 65% of the children surveyed were illiterates both boys and girls. Quite a large number of the working children—62% got only Rs. 3/- per day. The monthly earning of girls was much lower when compared to boys. Decidedly, the legal protection was rather nil which indirectly encourage intolerable working conditions for the growing child.

Immediately after the dawn of independence, there was an unprecedented upsurge of national feeling. It was like a mighty river bursting its dam and its water flooding all open space. Nothing could restrain the enthusiasm for national reconstruc-

12. p. 26 of the Report.
13. Pichoholiya, K.R. "Child Labour in a Metropolitan City (A Study of Ahmedabad), January 1980 (from Journal of Labour Economics Conference).

tion. Some of the zealous humanitarians looked towards children, as some had looked at the plight of women and Harijans and each vied with the other to do his utmost to improve prevailing conditions. The Indian Council for Child Welfare joined hands with the International Union for Child Welfare which had their liaison with the UNICEF, UNESCO, FAO & W.H.O. and they started an indepth study of child's problems. It was at once a national issue and attention was instantly fixed at the unfortunate child.

Only five years after independence an International Study Conference was held under the high patronage of the Government of India at Bombay between 5 to 12 December, 1952, and was internationally represented. It was an exploratory study with the objective of finding out areas of service needed by the child. Often it was child's health, child's education, care of the handicapped, social services and child welfare and maternity problems. The calling tune was coordinated efforts and pooling experiences. The then Prime Minister of India Pt. Jawaharlal Nehru referring to the Five Year Plan confessed that there was a chapter here or there related to child welfare, otherwise all was lost before the main focus on agriculture and industry. It was in this conference that Jawaharlal Nehru gave a mantric statement : 'It is the human being that counts, and if the human being counts, well, he counts much more as a child than as a grown up'.

The Conference was all sincerity, but it lacked a vision, a vision of the problems of the working child. Most regrettably, other conferences that ensued, as for example, The National Conference on Child Welfare, held at New Delhi, between 9 and 12 May 1956, National Seminar sponsored by ICCW at Hyderabad between 12-15 February 1964, entitled A National Policy for Children, and lastly, A seminar organised by International Children's Centre, Paris, and ICCW, New Delhi, at Madras in 1970, discussed matters relating to the Pre-school child and set their sights on the usual topics like child's health, nutrition, education, welfare and recreation programmes in urban and rural areas but not on child's exploitation in industry. Even 23 years after Independence, these seminars could not reach the fringe of working children's miseries, far less have a grip on them, although there existed protective and preventive laws. The laws failed the boys as they failed the girls in matters of dowry. Public awakening was wanting—that was and that is even now-the reason for the perpetuation of child's tribulations. But, it would not last for ever : change in political and social life is a part of natural social dynamics. Popular public journgls mounted their guns on the miserable plight of the 'economic', boys and girls of poor man's families. The deep mystical silence now roared and reverberated. Each journal brought to light new facets, new dimensions and new spheres where the muffled children were breathing hard with work and fatigue. Ultimately these guardians of the nation, the fearless sentinels of truth, came to the child's succour and forced intellectuals, administrators, philanthropists to save children from rushing to an early grave. Even law and voluntary organisations were goaded and provoked to join the issue without delay.

The eminent constitutional advocate Mr. Soli Sorabjee brought to light at a workshop meeting on child labour organized by the Indian Institute in New Delhi that there existed a Children Act (1938) providing protection to children but it has been futile since 'there was not a single court decision against anybody under the Employment of Children Act (1938).' He further remarked : "It was silly to believe that the employers would look after the children even if a law was made to this effect and was equally juvenile to think that the law would remain a temporary measure only towards a gradual phasing out of this evil' (Times of India, Aug. 10, 1986, New Delhi).

Emincnt Indian Journals, dailies and periodicals, discovered the snag in the laws in vogue and informed the people as a social educationist would do. This led to discussions in Lok

Sabha and Rajya Sabha which were meant to remove the snags. The Hindustan Times, New Delhi, dated 13th August 1987 reports an announcement in Rajya Sabha by the then State Labour Minister at the Centre Sri P.A. Sangma about a three point national policy on child labour to prevent exploitation, to rehabilitate, and to initiate positive action for children welfare. Then industries were initially taken to account where children were working in unhealthy conditions and the new project would cover about 30,000 children. Yet a member pointed out that these earning children would be put to a financial disadvantage which indeed needed attention of the law makers. Sri Sangma told the Rajya Sabha that the Government had accepted the social challenge. For this purpose enforcement of laws would be stepped up and even special enforcement staff might be deployed. The families of the child would be covered under the income and employment generating programmes as part of overall anti-poverty programmes. Formal and non-formal education and health care would be provided. The annual cost of the reformed 10 projacts would be Rs. 11 crores.

There will be a child labour project board for each project with the local collector as its chairman and with officials, non-officials and representatives of voluntary organisation as members to ensure coordination of the inputs by the various departments."

Writing on the same day, i.e. 13-8-1987, in the Times of India the two Columnists, Lotika Sarkar and Chanchal Sarkar referred to a speech by the Central Labour Minister Sri Virendra Patil made in 1983 in which he had said : "We are quite clear in our minds that we are not for the continuance of child labour. Government wants the total elimination of child labour. But it is not possible to have it immediately, it has to be eliminated gradually, and as speedily as possible". T. Anjaiah declared in May 1985 that the government was planning a comprehensive Act on Child Labour...."The

Employment of Children Act 1938 had envisaged certain punishments to the exploiters, although they were never used. The new Act sought more punishment, imprisonment, and enhanced fines, to enforce its mandatoriness, but all seemed to be tall talk and deft postponement. Virendra Patil himself confessed that the government was poor in implementation. Patil, Anjaiah and Sangma were vociferous in convincing the country that child labour would be eliminated in 10 years, but we are witness to its failure in 1989. Instead, situation has gone worse—we have descended the scale from child labour to Infant Labour. Children of 3½ years are reported to be working. They labour from 5 a.m. to 6/9 p.m. for a paltry sum of Rs. 2/- and Rs. 7/- a day. Things are still gloomy in Shivkasi where match industry flourishes along with crackers and fire works commodities. Little children are working in Bidi Industry also. Deformity of body, tuberclosis cases, other respiratory diseases are rampant among them. A cess is being proposed in the infamous industries to meet child labour costs in addition to their wages. The Columnists deprecate these steps and advocate stringent laws against employment of "the bottom-of-the-heap Indian Kids" who have never known childhood.

Being pressed hard the Centre asked the states to report on the prevailing conditions of child labour and on the available child welfare schemes. The government was soon informed that leave alone the Children Act, even the Minimum Wages Act, the Factories Act were not enforced properly. They stayed in paper only (Times of India, New Delhi 2-11-1987). The Hindustan Times, New Delhi, did not lag behind and wrote a leading article 'Child Labour Policy' on 14th August 1987 and mentioned pointedly 'the apathy of the government' towards child welfare, and bitterly complained of a joke committed on the people by promising a 'comprehensive' Child Labour Prohibition and Regulating Act 1986. Regulating the employment of children above the age of 12 years to fight poverty in selected areas of organised sector was more prominent in its violation then implementation. There was no enforcement machinery which enabled the employers to carry on as they wished. The vested interests perpetuate the ignominous acts until their arms are destroyed. Sadly enough the said Act of 1986 does not clearly define or describe the 'hazardous' jobs for children. Likewise, there is no regulating or Preventive Act for Children in the unorganized sector.

So much of din and bustle was bound to arouse immense public opinion. The languishing lot of about "300 children, comprising of rag pickers, porters, coolies, cooks in Dhabas, helpers in workshops, and shoe shine boys staged a rally from Jantarmanter to Boat Club in New Delhi on April 30, 1988. The object according to the Forum for Street and Working Children (FSWC), a voluntory organisation, was to create an awareness among the people on the miserable plight of about 18 million child workers below the age of 15".

The Child Labour Prohibition and Regulation Act of 1986 was discussed and a demand was repeated for the safeguard measures, viz, "provision for education, recreational facilities, adherence to minimum wages, weekly rest day, hygenic working conditions, and a ban on overtime that affects the health of the child worker". It was also decided that "the only way to ensure compliance with the Act is to make punishment for violations more stringent and incorporate a provision for surprise checks and establish a separate vigilance cell. With regard to the workers' interest, it should be made mandatory for all employers to take steps for the intellectual, vocational and educational well being and uplift of a child worker whether one is employed as a factory hand, a domestic servant, or a shop assistant". (The Hindusthan Times—C. Prabhakaran, New Delhi, 9th May 1988).

The idea of regulating child labour and child welfare schemes percolated to Bhagalpur also and a survey was conducted in August 1988. It revealed that 'a number of weavers are increasingly falling prey to various types of lung diseases', which were due to inhalation of small particles of silk. According to the Director of the Central Tassar Research Training Institute, Ranchi, Mr. S.S. Sinha, 'over 6000 silk weavers were suffering from heart and skin diseases in Bhagalpur'. The weavers were also prone to tuberculosis, the study said. The skin ailment arose from contact with dyeing chemicals and allied factors. (The Times of India, Patna, 1-8-88).

In a still earlier issue The Times of India, Patna, March 27, 1988 reported that Bhagalpur produces 50 to 80 lacs metres of Tassar Silk annually which is exported to Germany, France, U.S.A., Japan, U.K., Italy, Switzerland and Spain. Bihar produces 70 to 80 percent of the country's Tasaar Silk for which Bhagalpur is famous all the world over. Ansaris (Muslims) and Tantis (Hindus) are hundred percent engaged in the job of silk production. Children belonging to their family as well as from outside villages are engaged in silk manufacture on a large scale. But what impedes gross silk production is the frequent power trippings. The weavers rightly say that against a required supply of 23 MW needed for round the clock working of the power-loom, only 9 MW is supplied, that also with frequent power failures as a result of which the quality of the silk suffers. Naturally, wage payment to children gets a set back.

It is worth considering why children are not being cared for in our country inspite of many pious wishes. The main vehicle for child development in recent years has been the ICDS (Integrated Child Development Services) which is one of the Largest National Development Programme in India. But its impact on the rural and tribal children is yet to be established. Nobody bothers for children since they cannot bring votes nor can they protest. Even voluntary organisations speaking for them are on the wane (see the Times of India—Letter column 1-8-88).

Repetition is the hallmark of slogan shouting. Each paper considers writing about the deplorable conditions of working children, but it also cries hoarse about the apathy of the government, the people, and the parents to take up the cudgel. Preventive and Regulating laws are there only to be ignored. Sometimes a streak of light comes in the form of amendments and governments' proclamations to implement the laws, but these are like the voice 'sleep no more' 'murder, foul murder' is in air which we hear in Macbeth. One cannot deny that our children are living through slow death, murder at our own hands, even while we call them hopes of our future, pillars of our nation. We glorify children because they can be easily sacrificed. But is it not pitiable, grim and dark until we turn honest and give them their share of a happy, free like the air, life.

CHAPTER V

Methodology of this Study

THEORETICAL PERSPECTIVE ON RESEARCH METHODOLOGY

Academic research into a social problem is an alluring venture. When undertaken empirically it tends to yield substantive and convincing results. The conclusions arrived at can be used beneficially in reducing social disharmony. Indeed such research has to be scientific and systematic, revolving round a specific topic. The search for knoweldge begins with two presuppositions, viz, one—that the problem or the fact exists, and second, that the mystic veil surrounding it can be removed to get a vision of the hidden solution. The 'is-ness' of a fact, and the 'is-ness' of method co-exist like the child in the mother, and the mother in the child. What is required is the activisation of the instinct of inquisitveness : once stirred, the distant truth comes to hand—handy, ready for use in alleviating social tension.

Indeed, there are many routes open to the voyager. It is up to him to select the one that holds the greatest possibilities for him. It is also true that other routes will enrich his store of information, so being wise, he will not spurn any one of them. Instead, like a tactful warrior he will use his arsenal according to the item, place and the nature of his project. What Falstaff said in Henry IV holds true even today Sir "Discretion is the best part of valour, Sir".[1]

A valuable research is, therefore, a fountain of knowledge, as well as, an important source of providing guidelines for solving different business, governmental and social. They add to our knowledge equally well when we undertake conceptual research as in the realm of philosophy or factual as in the domain of history. The role of research in the field of applied economics, either related to a business or the gross national product has increased considerably in modern times, mostly as an aid to, and a source of, valuable information for both the people and the government. It helps in the formulation of a nation's economic policy. Consider the plight of the cultivators, the problems of big and small industries, working conditions of labourers and even child and female labour, trade union activities, the problem of distribution, even the size and nature of defence services, and we feel the necessity of in-depth research into these matters to enlighten both the people and the State. Allocation of national revenues depends entirely on such research which no government can overlook.

Karl Jaspers rightly said: "Whereas ancient science had the appearance of something completed, to which the notion of progress was not essential, modern science progresses into the infinite". Quest for more and more knowledge is the trait of the modern man. Thus he cannot sit silent over the happenings in the social sphere. Research, both extensive and intensive, has become a passion with social scientists. Marie Jahod correctly affirms: "The reasons for asking research questions are of two general kinds: Intellectual, based on the desire to know or understand for the satisfaction of knowing or understanding, and Practical, based on the desire

1. Shakespeare's Henry ; Act-V ; IV ; 120 Line.

to know for the sake of being able to do something better or more efficiently.... Historically, the scientific enterprise has been concerned both with knowledge for its own sake (Pure) and with knowledge for what it can contribute to practical concerns (applied). This double emphasis is perhaps especially, appropriate in the case of social science. On the one hand, its responsibility as a science is to develop a body of principles that make possible the understanding and prediction of the whole range of human interactions. On the other hand, because of its social orientation, it is increasingly being looked to for practical guidance in solving immediate problems of human relations."[2] Thus research is equally important for social scientists in studying social relationship and in seeking answers to various social problems."[3] Research becomes a part of decision-making process, step by step, even though it is not its primary aim.

Naturally, therefore, there may be many types of research. It may be Descriptive or Analytical. As tbe name suggests, Descriptive research may simply describe the state of affairs as it exists. When a researcher has no control over the variables, the researcher can only report what is happening. This is also known as Ex. Post Facto Research. It includes survey methods of all kinds. In Analytical research, the researcher has to use facts or informatios already available, and analyse these to make a critical evaluation of the material.

Secondly, there may be Applied or Fundamental Research. The fundamental research concentrates purely on generalising or theorising whereas applied research looks at seeking solutions of immediate problems prevailing in a society.

Thirdly, research may be centred round Quantitative or

2. Jahoda, Marie : Research Methods in Social Relations : p. 4 U.S.A., 1962.
3. Kothari, C.R., Research Methodology : Wiley Eastern Ltd. New Delhi, 1985 p. 9.

Qualitative discoveries. When we try to investigate into a pattern of human behaviour, we look into motivations and this forms the nucleus of qualitative research whereas, when we study the frequency of a social phenomenon, we express it in terms of quantity and it becomes quantitative research. This is more or less mathematical while the other is psychological research.

Conceptual versus Empirical research form another group of investigations. Conceptual is mostly abstract and philosophical, whereas Empirical is highly rational. "Empirical research is appropriate when proof is sought that certain variables affect other variables in some way. Evidence gathered through experiments or empirical studies is today considered to be the most powerful support possible for a given hypothesis."[4]

Researches may be of various other types as well. They may be 'one time or longitudinal', 'field-setting' or 'laboratory centred', 'clinical or diagnostic', 'exploratory or formalized', 'historical or geographical' and many others. In fact, all "researches inculcate scientific and inductive thinking and they promote the development of logical habits thinking and organisation."[5] But two things have always to be kept in mind. The one is the difference between research methods and research methodology, and the other is the melting away of all differences among research techniques. In actual process and progress, all techniques converge on each other and all barriers of difference vanish. Research methods mean all those methods or techniques used for conducting research. Briefly speaking research methods refer to the techniques the researcher use in their project. They also include the behaviour and instruments used in the process of collecting data, in establishing relationship between the data and the unknown conclusion

4. Ibid, p. 5.
5. Ibid, p. 7.

through statistical methods, and lastly, the methods used to evaluate, verify, and conclude the accuracy of the results obtained. Research methodology is a bigger term, something like a genus, whose species is research method. Research methodology is the way to systematically solve the research problem, for example, an architect is confronted with the problems of shape, size, number, location of doors, windows, roof etc. and he uses his tools of measurements and makes his decision. "Researcher not only need to know how to develop certain indices or tests, how to calculate the mean, the mode, the median, or the standard deviation of chi-square, how to apply particular research techniques, but they also need to know which of these methods or techniques, are relevant and which are not, and what would they mean and indicate and why. The researchers also need to understand the assumptions underlying various techniques and they need to know the criteria by which they can decide that certain techniques and procedures will be applicable to certain problems and others will not. All this means that it is necessary for the researcher to design his methodology for his problems as the same may differ from problem to problem."[6] In short research methodology is a scientific vision of the beginning and the end of a problem seen through the lens of techniques. Method may be individual and varying, but methodology is a collective name of the entire gamut of techniques.

Empirical method of research, being so vastly different from guess work or gossip, is evidently the most rigorous, impersonal, scientific, logical and objective process of investigation. It depends upon close evidence, relevant concepts, ethical neutrality, free from personal bias, and keeps an eye on objective considerations, as well as, future verification on scrutiny. External orderliness and internal consistency are its high water marks, its sterling quality. As such, the present researcher has cautiously valued the advantages and perils of empirical

6. Ibid, p. 11.

research before embarking on the formulation of her hypothesis. As such, the researcher has at the very outset singled out her problem of study, her area of interest and aspects of the subject matter after group discussion, visits to the area of concern, and after probing through all important literatures available on the subject.

Child Labour in Silk Industry of Bhagalpur is extensively prevalent inspite of government's manifold efforts to protect children from exploitation. Not that all government's measures are going invain, no, not at all, some of the measures are yielding good results and children are availing themselves of opportunities meant for their betterment. Yet, if poverty and illiteracy and concomitant factors exist, then child labour also exists as a consequence. Tragically enough, not much sociological study has been done regarding child labour, far less about Child Labour in Silk Industry. Practically, there is no reference available regarding child's participation in the Silk Industry of Bhagalpur. Of course, whatever has been done in this field is by psychologists and economists (to some extent), dealing with their mental behaviour and the problem of labour, management, and suitability in the industry. Child Labour in Bihar finds no mention in government's statistics a lacuna which needs immediate attention of the administration.

The present study on Child Labour in the Silk Industry of Bhagalpur is therefore, expected to reveal many unknown dimensions of children's lives from sociological point of view against the setting of Silk Industry in Bhagalpur. Traditionally, Bhagalpur is called a silk city for its manufacture and exports of several varieties of silk. It covers a big area from Nathnagar, Champanagar. Narga in Bhagalpur Municipal Corporation to the borders of Santhal Parganas in Mirzachowki and villages nearby. Yet silk manufacture and its sale centres flourish mainly in Nathnagar and Bhagalpur. Child labour constitutes a sizable proportion of the total labour engaged in the trade, especially in manufacturing processes.

Objective

The objectives of the present study are to analyse the life-pattern of these children, beginning from their family background, educational aspiration, occupational mobility to motivations and economic pulls and pushes. Along with these, conditions at working places, opportunities for entertainments and recreations, religious attitude, employer-employee relationship, safeties, job-satisfaction, securities in jobs, promotion and increase in wages and such other various problems along with the adequacy of governmental measures and children's ability to utilise them have been studied empirically. Since the dwelling unit is the locus of the initial socialization, great attention has been paid to the study of the living conditions of the children engaged in silk labour, and this includes the condition of the house, lavatories, bath-rooms (if any), electricity, clean drinking water, ventilation in living rooms, and also kitchen and meal habits. Not less important is the study of different forces that are operating outside and inside the society and influencing the children directly or indirectly. The pattern of the family to which the labouring child belongs is itself an indicator—family's size, decision-making process in the family, age at marriage, difference in the ages of the spouses, attitude towards customs, traditions, supersitions vis-a-vis the impact of media and the creeping change in social outlook as a consequence of modernization and urbanization. All these tend to include the educational level of the respondents (child-labour) because with the increase in the educational level, increase in occupational mobility, a sense of dignity of labour and trade and awareness of the happenings both in the country and outside. 'Drop out' cases of schools are cases of morbidity. They do not exhibit any zeal to improve their lot or adopt ways and mean to get out of social morass or financial catastrophe. Education also influences the employer-employee relationship taking cruelties lying down and the crash of the whip and abuses, are things of the past. What we finally gain is a vision of a long-range social change among the Child Labour in the Silk Industry at Bhagalpur. Quite often intellectual interests generate practical concerns and in the process give a glimpse of the problems that call for solution. In actual life, the final solution of a problem is a misnomer. The end of one problem suggests the beginning of another, and thus the society exists on the wheel of time. But luckily there is a relieving factor embedded in each obstacle which points to its solution.

Hypothesis

The hypothesis the researcher proposed to verify are given below :

(i) Children engaged in the Silk Industry of Bhagalpur form the most exploited class of labour.

(ii) Attitudinal structure of the working children in the silk industry of Bhagalpur differed from other working children engaged elsewhere.

(iii) The socio-economic conditions exert profound influence on the personality of these children.

(iv) The children engaged in silk industry of Bhagalpur do specialised work but neither are they given the privilege enjoyed by other labourers in this industry, nor are they supposed to be indispensible.

(v) The legislative measures by the Government, protecting child labour, do not reach them.

(vi) People's awareness of the children's Act is miserably low.

Each hypothesis has a seed of the redeeming element which is the task of the researcher to discover and implement. Cohen and Nagel (1934) rightly suggest that "we cannot take a single step forward in any enquiry unless we begin with a suggested explanation or solution of the difficulty which originated it. Such tentative explanations are suggested to us by something in the subject matter and by our previous knowledge when they are formulated as propositions, they are called hypothesis."

"The function of a hypothesis is to direct our search for the order among facts. The suggestions formulated in the hypothesis may be solutions to the problem. Whether they are, is the task of the enquiry..."[7]

Universe, Setting and Sample

Thus devising samples from population stratum and describing setting of the population as a backdrop against which all investigations have to move are essential ingradients of an empirical research. The setting is the society from which individuals and groups concerned with research projects make the sample. If the setting is the locale, the stratum of the people become our universe and the units selected from the universe the sample for the proposed study. They become our respondents. It is among them that we live and breathe, enquire and collect honey of wisdom and knowledge like the sagacious bee. In fact, the universe supplies us the real sample we want to encounter.

In the present case our setting is Bhagalpur city and our universe is the working children in the silk industry round Nathnagar, Champanagar, Murgiachak, Bhagalpur City, Bhikhanpur, Mozahidpur, Moulnachak, Sarai & Barahpura, all lying in the Municipal Corporation area of Bhagalpur City. In all these muhallas the predominant population is of weavers both Hindus and Muslims engaged in powerloom and handloom manufacture of silk. Large numbers of children are found quietly serving the silk industry in these areas. Since the researcher has spent a major part of her childhood in the

7. Cohen, M.R. and E. Nagel, An Introduction to Logic and Ssientific Method, Harcourt, 1934—Quoted in Jahoda's Research, Methods in Social Relation, op. cit. p. 35.

central locality of Nathnagar and Champanagar she has witnessed the children working at handlooms and powerlooms with curiosity and interest. The choice of 'Child Labour in Silk Industry at Bhagalpur' as a social study, came to her naturally and she has witnessed the pleasures and pains, the vice and virtue rotating round the children working on the looms.

Bhagalpur city is situated at North Latitude 24°, 30′ and 25° 30′ and East Longitude 86°30′ and 87°30′ in the state of Bihar (North India). It is an ancient city, the capital town of Anga Pradesh, referred to in the Atharva Veda (one of the oldest Hindu Scriptures), Gopatha Brahmana, Aiteraya Brahmana, the Apastamba Srauta Sutra, the Valmiki Ramayana, the Mahabharata, Hari Vamsa Purana, Greek records of Megasthenes, and Buddhist and Jainese texts. Famous Travellers like Fa-Hien (405-411 AD), Hiuen Tsang (629-645 AD) also visited this hallowed place. Mention may be found in Alauddin Khilji's commercial records, in Ain-i-Akbari's political report[8] and in a tomb inscription of Ibadulleh Khwaza Ahmed, resident of Samarkand, and a founder of Kudsiul Alkab Sahabzada Alam Mian Shah Parviz Jehangir dated Hizri 1032"[9]. As we turn through the pages of history, we find Cleveland connected with Bhagalpur, the one for whom Burke had the highest eulogy in British Parliament, and Governor Warren Hastings, whom Burke had openly indicted in the same Parliament for his excesses. In course of time Bhagalpur city became a secret resort of Indian militant nationalists, a place for frequent visits of Mahatma Gandhi, Rajendra Prasad, Jawaharlal Nehru, Sarojini Naidu and others. The place become sacred with the touch of Sri Aurobindo's father, and Sarat Chandra Chatterjee, Mahadevi Verma, Dinkar, Subhas Chandra Bose and others. In a way, the tradition of its glory lies unbroken through the centuries

8. Todarmal came to Bhagalpur in 1580.
9. The Tomb is on the banks of the River Jamuna in Champanagar.

comprising of over three thousand years. All in all these eras, the tradition of silk manufacture also lies continuous and unbroken.[10]

Bhagalpur city today is slowly moving on the road to modernization. It has a number of schools and colleges, even vocational college of national importance and great public utility under Bhagalpur University, viz, Jawaharlal Nehru Medical College, Sabour Agriculture College, Engineering College, Silk and Textile Training School (at Nathnagar), Science and Arts Colleges for Men and Women. A well connected rail-road system, All India Radio Station and a TV relay centre, Post Office with Tele-communication, Hospitals, Nursing Homes, Kindergarten and plenty of children's schools, and a Provincial Police Constable Training School are Bhagalpur's plus points towards urbanization. It is expected that a National Thermal Power Corporation, and a road bridge across the Ganges will soon be coming up, giving it more energy for industry and easy accessibility to North Bihar and Assam. Trade is bound to develop with these measures in the offign, and naturally more opportunities for employment. Even Tourism shall get a boost for the undying charm of Vikramshila University and Karnagarh on the eastern and western fringes of Bhagalpur.

While agriculture is the mainstay of people, silk industry is richly patronised, first by the weavers themselves and second, by the Government. According to 1981 census, the total population of the city is 2,25,062 out of which 1,22,485 males and 1,02,577 are females and household are about 32,000. The area of Bhagalpur city is 30.17 km which is divided into 37 wards. The city stretches about 10 km from North to South and about 25 km from East to West. In the north of the city flows the holy Ganges, and in the South West, there is

10. Summarised from a research paper of Dr. S.P. Sinha, Pro-Vice Chancellor of Mandar Vidyapith, Bhagalpur. For details of Anga's antiquity his paper may be read with pleasure and profit.

the branch of Chandan river meeting the Ganges at Nathnagar. Plenty of prosperous villages flourish on the banks of the river which are inhabited by peaceful people of all communities. Hindus are in majority, but the greatest minority is of the Muslims, then come Jains, Sikhs, Christians etc. Sometimes past, there were some Jews also, but now there is none.

Urban community is multi-lingual, so is Bhagalpur. Apart from Hindi and Urdu, Bengali also spoken here. Marwari language, Bhojpuri, Magadi and Maithili are in use just as Santhali language. But the main dialect (labouring for the status of a language) is cheka-cheki or Angika which is spoken predominantly and is used and understood by the indigenous as well as the immigrant population of Bhagalpur. Yet, inspite of this richness, literacy rate is quite small. Out of a population of 2,25,602 only 78,928 males and 43,977 females are enumerated as literate. If in a total population of a city, (not to talk of rural area) 50% remain illiterate, poverty line must remain sufficiently high to cover more and more people under its banner. Bhagalpur city, therefore, presents a picture of people struggling to eke out a living—and in the process child labour becomes an essential consequence, an unavoidable vice, an inevitable destiny.

The formulation of a hypothesis—leads the investigator to the designing of samples. Samples have to be designed in such a way that they yield accurate information with a minimum amount of research effort. Statistical considerations in presenting the pictures of a defined group of people help us to reach near-accurate and reliable description of the attitudes and behaviour of the members involved. More often than not, a sample of the population of an area to be studied is sufficient. It has to be borne in mind at this time that we would be squandering men, money and time in dealing over a whole population which often comprises of diverse communities and diverse occupations. As such social investigation are focussed at population stratum and not the whole population. Social researches cannot be equated with census duty. Therefore, according to Isidor Chien: "when we select some of the elements with the intention of finding out something about the population from which they are taken, we refer to that group of elements as a sample."[11] This is done with a confidence that what we find about the sample is true of the population as a whole, just as one grain of cooked rice speaks about the entire rice in the cooking pan. We rightly begin sampling with a high hope of probability and a rich crop of discovery.

Keeping in mind that sample is a small number of individuals drawn from the larger population and the above mentioned facts about the size and reliability of the sample, it was considered logical to follow the rules of purposive sampling method here. Thus a sample of 250 respondents from the children employed in silk industry of Bhagalpur was drawn to serve adequately the purpose of the study. It is homogenous sample because it constitutes only the children employed in the silk industry. But, on the other hand, since the respondents differ among themselves in regard to their background, characteristics like family and social upbringing, the sample may be considered as heterogenous in character. As a matter of fact, individuals even through living in the same condition and society, differ in their socio-economic conditions. The socio-economic conditions exert profound influence on the personality, on the thinking and acting capability of individuals. Dubey rightly remarked that, "In the formation of human personality, as well as, in the moulding of the thoughts and actions social surroundings play a considerable role."[12] In sociological study therefore, the imporatnce is given to the

11. Jahoda Marie et al—"Researeh Methods In Social Relations". Quoted from Isidor Chien, Appendix B, Ny. 1951. p. 509.
12. S.M. Dubey, "Social Mobiliiy Vmong the Professions," (Bombay Popular Prakashan, (1972) p. 59.

socio-economic background of respondents and are taken up as variables for empirical analysis.

We, therefore, need to present a vivid portrayal of the socio-economic profile of our respondents to complete an investigative empirical study.

SOCIO-ECONOMIC PROFILE OF THE RESPONDENTS

Area of Residence

Since the study is aimed at presenting a comparative appraisal of status, and socio-economic problems of child labour in silk industry of Bhagalpur it is inevitable to select setting and sample from both rural and urban areas around Bhagalpur city :

In the rural areas the unit of silk industry or powerlooms or handlooms are rare. Thus, for the need of intensive study the respondents were asked to explain about their original native residence. 128 respondents i.e., 51.20 per cent of the total sample reported that they belong to urban areas. Rest 48.80 per cent numbering 122 were coming from rural area. (Table 1).

TABLE 1

Respondents and Their Place of Birth

Place of birth	*No.*	*Percent*
Rural	122	48.80
Urban	128	51.20
Total	250	100.00

Respondents and Age-group

Only such children who were engaged in various types of works in silk industry are included in this sample. Therefore, all respondents in this sample were below 14 years of age, but even among them difference is marked. The largest number 52.80 percent respondents belonged to the age group of 11-13 years, whereas, the lowest number 3.60 per cent belonged to 5-7 years of age group. 22.80 per cent and 20.80 per cent respondents belonged to the age group below 14 years and 8-10 years of age group respectively. The age group of rural and urban respondents also reflected a greater similarity. (see Table 2).

TABLE 2

Distribution of Respondents According to their Age Groups

Variables	*No.*	*Percent*
Age group		
5—7	9	3.60
8—10	52	20.80
11—13	132	25.80
Urto—14	57	22.80
Total	250	100.00

Educational Level of Respondents and their Parents

Classification of respondents on the basis of educational level in Table 3 reveals that a majority of 62.80 percent respondents had received primary education, whereas, the least proportion of 10.40 per cent among them were educated upto middle standard. 26.80 per cent among them were illiterate, having never come into contact with alphabets.

To show the influence of parent's education on their children the educational level of parents were also taken and presented in the statistical form. The data collected in this connection reveal that the parents illiteracy or lower education is a hinderance to the child's proper socialization. According to the data collected the vast majority of 64.80% (Father) and 95.60 per cent (Mother) were illiterate (see detail break up of data in Table 3).

Occupational Structure of Respondents and Their Parents

Parent's occupations influence their children very much as regards status, sense of comfort, etc. With this view the respondents and their parents were classified in accordance with their occupation in which they were found engaged at the time of field investigation. It is clear that our sample comprises only of the children engaged in silk industry. In other words they all belong to private firms. But as regards their parents large occupation variation is found. Our data reveal that a vast majority of 46 per cent and the lowest 3.20 per cent (father) are found engaged in agriculture and government inferior service respectively. Twenty-six percent were manual workers. 18.40 per cent were private service holders and the rest 6.40 percent were engaged in their own business, like vegetable vending, cosmetics vending, rag-tag-picking, cloth vending and mason labour.

Every Indian woman is primarily a house-wife because irrespective of her level of literacy and occupation she has to perform the house-hold duties. However the respondent's mothers are classified in accordance with their occupation in which they were found engaged. Data in this context reveal that an overwhelming majority of 58.80 percent of them were housewives. The next larger group 22.80 per cent were manual workers. 11.20 per cent reported that they perform agricultural labour. Rest 4.80 per cent and 2.40 per cent were found in business and private service respectively like maid servants, cooks, house construction labour, vegetable vending etc. (Table 4).

TABLE 3

Distribution of Respondents' and Their Parents According to Their Education

Variable	Child Respondents		Father		Mother	
	No	Percent	No	Percent	No	Percent
Education						
Illiterate	67	26.80	162	64.80	239	95.60
Primary	157	62.80	54	21.60	11	4.40
Middle	26	10.40	29	11.60	—	—
Matric	—	—	4	1.60	—	—
Intermediate and above	—	—	1	0.40	—	—
Total	250	100.00	250	100.00	250	100.00

TABLE 4

Distribution of Respondents and Their Parents According to Their Occupations

Occupation	*Respondents*		*Father*		*Mother*	
	No	*Percent*	*No*	*Percent*	*No*	*Percent*
Service						
(a) Private	250	100.00	46	18.40	6	2.40
(b) Govt.	—	—	8	3.20	—	—
Agriculture Labour	—	—	115	46.00	28	11.20
Manual Worker	—	—	65	26.00	57	22.80
Business	—	—	16	6.40	12	4.80
House-Wife	—	—	—	—	147	58.80
Total	250	100.00	250	100.00	250	100.00

Income

Income is the index of individual's economic condition. Respondents relating to the sample belonged to four different annual income groups of family. Keeping in view the generally accepted criteria of categorization into different income strata we can say that the people who earn Rs. 18,000/- yearly belong to lower income group, Rs. 18,001/- to 30,000/- belong to middle income group and above Rs. 30,000/- annually belong to upper income group. The respondent's income was not exclusively taken up for classifying their income strata because respondents personal income is not sufficient even for himself and here we are concerned with family income. However, data in Table 5 reveal that majority of respondents 46.40 per cent (Rs. 5,001/- — 10,000/-), 36.80 per cent (upto Rs. 5,000/-) and 11.20 per cent (Rs. 10,001/- — 15,001/-) were the members of lower income group families, whereas, the lowest 5.60 per cent reported their membership in middle income group. Not even a single respondent reported that he belongs to upper ineome group. (Table 5).

TABLE 5

Respondents and Their Yearly Family Income

Income Group (Yearly in Rupees)	*No*	*Percent*
Upto 5,000/-	92	36.80
5,001/- — 10,000/-	116	46.40
10,001/- — 15,000/-	28	11.20
15,001/- and above	14	56.0
Total	250	100.00

Type of Family

Our sample respondents belonged to different types of families. The largest number of them were members of nuclear family (65.60 per cent), whereas the lowest proportion of 13.20 per cent belonged to joint family, and the remaining 21.20 per cent respondents were the members of extended family. (Table 6).

TABLE 6

Distribution of Respondents According to Their Type of Family

Type of Family	*No.*	*Percent*
Joint family	33	13.20
Extended family	53	21.20
Nuclear family	164	65.60
Total	250	100.00

Caste

It does not need elaboration that the unique institution of caste has tremendous impact upon the members of Indian Society. Almost every aspect of an individual's life gets shaped by the ideology and rules of castes. However, it is not true that caste form does not prevail among non-Hindu. We find some sort of stratification among Muslim and other religious groups. So, for the sake of deep study the respondents were classified into four broad caste groups—Upper caste, Lower but not backward, Backwards and lastly scheduled castes group. Data in regard to castewise distribution of respondents find mention in Table 7. It is revealed that the largest number 66.40 per cent respondents belonged to Scheduled Caste, whereas, the next larger number 15.60 per cent were members of Backward Castes. But the number of respondents belonging to upper caste group 5.20 per cent was the lowest in the sample. 12.80 per cent was the number of lower but not backward caste group.

TABLE 7

Respondents Number and Percentage According to Their Castes

Variable	*No.*	*Percent*
Upper Caste	13	5.20
Lower but not Backward	32	12.80
Backwards	39	15.60
Scheduled Castes	166	66.40
Total	250	100.00

Religion

It would be pertinent to mention here that all the respondents of sample were taken from the Silk Industry of Bhagalpur City. Data in this regard are very clear. The vast majority of 81.60 per cent were of Muslim Community and the rest 18.40 per cent were of Hindu Community. It is so because of the fact that the trait of weaving is more popular among Muslims than the Hindus.

TABLE 8

Respondents and Their Religions

Religion	*No.*	*Percent*
Hindu	46	18.40
Muslim	204	81.60
Total	250	100.00

Sex-wise Classification

Children found engaged in silk industry were both boys and girls. But it is necessary to mention here that the girls engaged in this industry were local and below the age of 10 years. In the study sample their number was low in comparison to boys. As the data reveal that only 10.80 per cent among them were girls and rest 89.20 per cent were boys.

TABLE 9

Sex-wise Distribution of Respondents

Sex	*No.*	*Percent*
Boys	223	89.20
Girls	27	10.80
Total	250	100.00

With this setting of Bhagalpur City, and a description of the 'Sample' mentioned above, the researcher has designed her tools and techniques which are in vogue among sociological researchers. As a rule, the formulation of the problem should be followed by data collection through specific and suitable methods. Each of the various methods—observation, interviewing, questionnaires, projective techniques, examination of records and others, has its own advantages and limitations and the researcher has to pick and choose the most relevant among them. In the present case, therefore, the interview schedule seemed to be the only technique suitable for data collection. The sample population represent mostly the illiterate or semi-literate children. Hence the questionnaire though printed in English and Hindi simultaneously could not be administered to them straightway. A direct interview could be the only way out to solve the impasse. Interview schedule alone could fetch the information about the labouring children's feelings, beliefs, motivation and future plans. The same schedule has been administered in all the localities and each question has been explained repetitively in Hindi, *Hindustani and*

Angika to each respondents. Consequently it has taken nearly six months from the researcher to complete data collection.

The first part of the schedule concerns itself with the personal identification and respondent's personal informations, such as, name, age, address, religion and family description. Educational particulars of the child are also included therein. (from Q 1 to Q 9). This is followed by the educational particulars of parents and other family members, as well as, their economic status (Question 10-12) suggesting indirectly occupational mobility. But the main battle-lines are seen drawn from (question 13-17) when the respondents were asked in detail about their employers, employment particulars and employer-employee relation. Along with these, informations were elicited from the respondents on working hour, working conditions (place of work, total time spent, ventilation, meals etc.) and finally wage payment schemes. Some more personal questions were aimed at the respondents regarding their utility of wages, job-satisfaction and alternatives when they are out of work, security in jobs etc. (Q. 18 to Q. 23). Some open ended questions were formulated in the form of statements and the respondents were offered full liberty to agree or disagree with them. These were of generalised character such as the status of a working child in the family (Q. 24), their personal habits and hobbies, religious inclinations, and future plans (Q. 25-32). Direct interview and spontaneous conversation proved extremely helpful in the present study, as there could be no room for bias, unreliability and preconceived notions or ambiguity. Obviously, in the course of field work a good rapport was established both with the working child and his employer, and it was with their help that various facts were gathered through spontaneous, heart to heart and on the spot conversation in a cooperative spirit. The helpers in the field work, technically called investigators, were especially instructed to avoid confrontation and to extend full support to the respondents by clearing all situations of suspicion or shyness or even fear. Every talk took place therefore in an atmosphere of amicability and friendliness. It was impressed on them that this was an academic investigations, not administrative and in the end, the result of investigations might bring to them good fruits and rewards in the shape of healthy measures from the Government.

Secondary sources, apart from direct interviews, have their own merits and their assistance in forming a hypothesis or designing a research problem is immeasurable. Our country's journalistic standards are high—strictly objective—and they leave no problem untouched. They take as much interest in publishing the findings of Amnesty International, as in flashing boldy the findings of International Labour Organizations, reports of United Nations Organizations and World Health Organizations or the rising trends in the price of sugar, rice, oil seeds or the menace of rats in food godowns or kidnapping of man, woman or child. Journalism today is an industry, as such it is descriptive, exploratory and investigative. It is also enlightening and educatlve. Child labour as a problem has caught the attention of magazines issued monthly or newspapers published daily. Their reports have been comprehensively informative, but space and policy would not allow them to be producing in depth studies which is, indeed, the work of an industrious research project. Yet, they are the path finders or torch bearers of the society and the present study is enormously indebted to them. Census Reports, District Gazetteers, Statistical Publications, and above all, personal observation of social problems are immensely valuable source-materials and the researcher is glad to accept their role in preparing the research design, tools and techniques. Simultaneously, one cannot ignore the contribution of Television and Radio which send out news on all matters of public importance.

After the completion of field work and collection of data, the information so received were checked. Since the researcher had all along accompanied her team of workers, she had laboriously and meticulously put the questions in Hindi or the local dialect of chika-chiki (Angika). Chances of errors were few or none. Therefore, the next step was to examine the data by using appropriate statistical techniques, such as averages and percentages and mean. The independent variable 'child labour' has remained constant because all the informations collected were about child's labour in silk industry of Bhagalpur. This envisaged the application of simple statistical tools where results are portrayed in the different tables in different chapters. The researcher has already clarified the connotation and denotation of the essential terms constituting the problem, viz, child, labour, silk industry, and Bhagalpur. For utility sake and for immediacy of appeal, it may be repeated that a child is a person of both sexes between the age group 04-14. Child labour is the employment of a child in any industry, big and small, through which the child earns his bread and the industry profits out of his/her labours. Silk Industry is, in fact, the effort to produce linen out of silk fibres drawn from cocoons, and Bhagalpur is a Divisional Town in Bihar where silk industry flourishes from times of yore.

We have thus discussed the whole gamut of methodology from the formulation of the hypothesis 'child labour in the Silk Industry of Bhagalpur' to sample, setting, universe, and collection of data. We have also indicated the statistical processes applied in preparing the tables which offer us enormous information about the child engaged in the silk industry, the character of his labour, relations between employer and the employee, child's future, as well as the diffferent aspects of silk industry at Bhagalpur.

CHAPTER VI

Analysis and Interpretation of Data

Of late child labour has caught the attention of sympathetic people in our country. Silk Industry in Bhagalpur is an informal sector of production where working conditions are harsh, especially for children. Yet it is only a segment of a scenario that is painful and deeply agonising. We talk too much of labour welfare and its international solidarity, but even in the year 1990 we have not resolved all the labour issues. Rightly does the leading article in the *Times of India*[1] mention two gruesome facts—one, "Specifically in the Indian context it is obvious that the working class has only just begun its long and arduous journey towards securing even the rights given to by law. It is only a miniscule segment of Indian workers which is actually covered by the security provided by such industrial relations legislation as it exists. The so-called organised sector is only a small part of industry and even within that, all workers are not unionised." And secondly, as the editor proceeds, "The shame of our 20 million working children, deprived of their childhood in sweetshops in many hazardous industries, is noted from time to time but more ingenuity is employed to

1. *The Times of India*, Patna, Dated 3rd May, 1990.

cover up the gruesome facts than in ameliorating their conditions and giving them what is owed to them by any civilized society. The International Labour Organization (ILO) has also noted that "while child labour has decreased dramatically in industry in recent years, it is still widespread in third world agriculture, the urban informal sector and domestic service."[2] And the reason for the continuation of such heinous practice is that child labour is most hidden from public scrutiny and their existence is nobody's concern. Silk industry in Bhagalpur involving a large number of children is likewise seen but unnoticed, more so because they include unpaid employees in family owned business. Child labour on hire and family child labour get so much intermixed in Bhagalpur Silk Industry that people do not labour to make a distinction between them and they think them off together as nothlng unusual or exploitative. In this chapter while we do not attempt at separating the two, the family child labour and the child labour on wages, but we, instead, try to bring out the different jobs they are required to perform, which eats away their childhood and leaves them on the brink of decay, physically and intellectually. Yet it is the child's hands that prepare the yarns to be woven into fanciful and fascinating patterns of silk fabric. We will, therefore, witness in this chapter what contribution the child makes to silk industry, as well as, closely look into the child's occupational status, their opinion and perception, their desires and demands through series of interviews and regular interview schedule. In empirical studies figures must speak for facts which need be organised, sifted, screened and then placed on the table.

First of all, we present a comprehensive description of works done by child labour in the manufacture of silk. We can broadly, categorise them under three head, viz.

2. Ibid, p. 5.

1. Primary work,
2. Secondary, work, and
3. Final work.

Primary Work

While preparing the silk fabric some works fall in this category, e.g., we begin by purchasing silk yarn of different classes from wholesale dealers or government agencies. The commodity so purchased is raw silk. Now it has to be dyed by the 'dyeing master', an expert in chemical colouring. He prepares the dye and the child labour is asked to dip the raw yarn in the dyeing tub. Here the child comes face to face with certain debilitating effects of chemicals but where child labour is cheap and available in thousands such vicissitudes go uncared for. When the yarn has been soaked and has caught the desired colour, children are called upon to put it on wooden shafts or bamboo hangers in the sun. It is now dried and the yarn is ready for spinning, yet before it goes upon the loom, it has to be reeled on NARI and BAI. NARI and BAI are just 6" long hollow wooden implement which take the yarn on them by a process of reeling through a spinning wheel or a charkha. Preparing the NARI and BAI is the second primary work for the child to perform.

Secondary Work

After the NARI and BAI are ready, CHAPTI is prepared. CHAPTI is a drum-like wooden appliance of wide girth with iron rim at both ends. This is used both in Handlooms and Powerloooms. Its length varies between 8' and 9' and yarn is rolled over it. The loom is fed with yarns from this CHAPTI which is also called BEAM.

Chapti, Beam and RACCH are now connected by yarns duly counted. RACCH is a rectangular wooden or steel frame of the same length as the Beam or Chapti and is filled with small iron spokes through which passes the yarn. It is connected to the shuttle and is pressed outwards to inwards to bring Nari and

Bai yarns passing as wefts in the shuttle in correct order. This helps the linen to be smooth and strong and tight, otherwise it would be loose and straggling.

Final Work

Now the Chapti, Beam and Reed or Racch are placed in final position on the loom (both Handloom and Powerloom) and the shuttle is ready to sing its song of manufacture with the help of Nari and Bai. Here sits the weaver, expert in his trade, highly experienced, singing hymns of creation (सृष्टि) and decay (जीर्ण) both symbolised through the silk linen. But before the master craftsman sits over his work, the entire pieparatory arrangement is done by the child labour.

Since the investigator personally observed the children at work, she was tempted to ask some interesting questions to them. What is your contribution in silk industry ? Give particulars please.

The data in Table 1 reveal that 17.60% of the children were found engaged in preparing Nari and Bai. Indeed this is an easy job, not strenuous, but what a pity if children between the age group of 5-6 years or utmost 7 years are found squatting in a posture that ultimately becomes tiring and a burden on nerves! About 66 out of 250 respondents, which comes to about 26.40 percent were engaged in other manual works concerned with the loom. 22.40% and 16% reported that they operated the spinning wheel and the looms. These respondents were in the age-group of 11-13 years, that is below 14 years. Children between 5-7 years or 8-10 years were not found on these jobs because that would be an impossible feat for them. Even then the work was in fact hard and burdensome for the age-group labourers of 11-13 years. The work needed concentration, deft handling and technical skill. Table 1 offers the picture of hazardous works being done by children, hazardous when related to their age, physical and mental capacity. To add to this, the hours of labour are extensive and harmful. It is not

TABLE 1

Children and Their Work in Silk Industry

Work	*AGE GROUP* 5-7 N.	5-7 P.	8-10 N.	8-10 P.	11-13 N.	11-13 P.	Upto 14 N.	Upto 14 P.	*Total* N.	*Total* P.
To prepare Nari	7	77.78	18	34.62	14	10.61	5	8.77	44	17.60
To collect waste yarn			22	42.31	15	11.36	7	12.28	44	17.60
To operate spinning wheel					36	28.27	20	35.09	56	22.40
To operate loom					19	14.39	21	36.84	40	16.00
Extra work	2	21.22	12	23.07	48	36.37	4	7.02	66	26.40
Total	9	100.00	52	100.00	132	100.00	57	100.00	250	100.00

for on hour or two, instead, the child is on the job all day long. Unluckily, therefore, while the law ordains that no child below the age of fourteen shall bc employed or permitted to work in any workshop[3], yet the Bhagalpur Silk Industry presents a picture of contradiction or violation of the Act.

The sccond question that naturally interested the researcher was : 'How many hours you work in the Factory ? The answers elicited from the respondents were extremely painful. They show, as in in Table 2 below that they are like "dumb-driven cattle" whose voice can never be heard, whose groans melt in the air like cries in the wilderness.

The figures obtaincd and placed above reveal that a great majority of 50.80% respondents worked from 8 in the morning to 6 in the evening. Among them 65.15 percent and 61.54 percent belong to the age group of 11 to 13 years, and 8 to 10 years respectively. They have half an hour interval for lunch or leisure at will, but it goes without emphasising that such long hours of work are arduous and baneful to the health of the children. Only 34.80% respondents gave out that their duty hour is from 10 am. to 8 pm. and 14.40% narrated that they work from 8 am to 4 pm. in the factory.

The surroundings where children work as labour force in the Silk Industry of Bhagalpur is of great social concern for the researcher. It is not alone burdensome work that has a lethal effect upon the child, but also the conditions, he works in, viz. sanitation, fresh air and potable water availability, cleanliness of the floor and the room, as well as, general environmental make-up of the place of work. These contribute to any workman's health, leave alone the child. Even the law is clear and emphatic about hours of work, compulsory weekly rest and the sanitation of the workhouse. As such, the researcher brought out three questions before the respondents.

3. Agrawal, Lakshman Das : Labour Minor Acts, Ram Narayan Lal Beni Prasad, Law Publishers, Allahabad, 1987, p. 14.

TABLE 2

Children and Hours of Work

Age-Group	*Time of work*						*Total*	
	8 AM—4 PM		*8 AM—6 PM*		*10 AM—8 PM*			
	N.	*P.*	*N.*	*P.*	*N.*	*P.*	*N.*	*P.*
5—7	6	66.67	2	22.22	1	11.11	9	100.00
8—10	9	17.31	32	61.54	11	21.15	52	100.00
11—13	19	14.39	86	65.15	27	20.46	132	100.00
Up to 14	2	3.51	7	12.28	48	84.21	57	100.00
Total	36	14.40	127	50.80	87	34.80	250	100.00

The first question was—How do you perform your work? Standing or sitting or both? Data collected in this regard revealed that a majority of workers viz, 37.60% perform their work standing for hours. The nature of the work is such that they cannot sit even for a while, naturally, it is a very difficult job which a child fulfils. Along with them 35.20% gave out that they work both sitting and standing according to their jobs on hand. 27.20 percent opined that they work mostly sitting, like preparing Nari and Bai.

Working in ill-ventilated and dark hovels takes its toll on the children. Diseases of the lungs and visual deficiencies follow such working conditions. To compound with them is the lack of adequate remuneration, complete absence of compensatory allowances or medical aid, very high cost of medical treatment or possibility of sick leave, for once a child is off his job, he has no guarantee of being reinstated. Pledging of a child into labour is mostly the result of poverty of the parents. The sick child is thrown to his own fate, abandoned, hopelessly irretrievable. But he pays the penalty of unhygenic condition he has to work under, and the sub-human upkeep of the work-houses due to the illiteracy of the master. Naturally, the second question that was raised before the respondents was—"Is the place of your work neat, clean, or unhygenic? A vast majority of the respondents, that is 86.40% unhesitatingly reported that they work in completely unhygenic conditions, inimical to their health and longevity. Only 13.60% respoun-dents were lucky enough to work in ventilated and clean surren-dings, which looked satisfactory to them, but was, in fact, only a bit better off than the unhygenic ones.

This brought the investigator is to subsidiary question : Do they get enough water and light where they work? Here the investigator observed that all the ancilliary works are done during day hours and in open light. The scarcity of power hits the silk production, but not the miscellaneous works related to the final job. Hence the light peeping through the window or lustily spread out on the varendahs were good enough for the working child. Of course, these children never had the benefit of electric fans : it would be luxury beyond their dreams. But what is noticeable is this that the houses of the weavers are mostly antiquated, dingy, foul-smelling, and devoid of natural light and air. Water supply in Bihar's towns is erratic and undepenable. Walls are not common in the muhallas of weavers. The weavers have to depend on the municipal water supply, just as they depend on the Electric Supply Office for the required energy for running the Powerlooms or having lights in their dwelling places. Naturally 79.60 percent of the respondents said that they do not get enongh water and light to meet their requirements in the factory. Quite a good amount of water is required for dyeing the yarn, which is scarce leading to a drop in annual silk manufacture. About 20.40% stated that their requirement of water and light is met agreeably. These can be seen in Table 3 placed below :

TABLE 3

Some Informations About Place of Work

			No.	*Percent*
(i)	How do you perform your work ?			
	(a)	Standing	94	37.66
	(b)	Sitting	68	27.20
	(c)	Both	88	35.20
		Total	250	100.00
(ii)	Is the place of work neat and clean or unhygenic ?			
	(a)	Neat and clean	34	13.60
	(b)	Unhygenic	216	86.40
	Total		250	100.00

(Contd.)

(iii)	Do you have enough water and light where you work		
	(a) Yes	51	20.40
	(b) No	199	79.60
	Total	250	100.00

We can deduce from the above data that the child labour employed in the silk industry of Bhagalpur lives and works in adverse circumstances, insalubrious surrounding and unhygenic condition which tells upon their physical and moral health.

Hours of works and Leisure

Every civilized country has a realization of the values of leisure in promoting work. Man is not machine. Work becomes monotonous and boring until it is adequately relieved by leisure. Leisure becomes lunch-time, gossip time and amusement or recreational hour. It replenishes lost energy of the labourer and refreshes them. Labourers Act, Factories Act, both recommend daily leisure, weekly off days, holidays and earned leave. These are meant to help the workmen to recoup their energy and keep up their outputs. If however, this is denied for one reason or another, it will be tyranny, intolerable in modern times. Yet in Bhagalpur silk industry, such lack of leisure is not unknown. Of course, political enlightenment of the people, even including child labour, has brought to them the consciousness that leisure is their right. Incidentally, however, this was noticed that child-labour on hire got only 30 mts leisure or no leisure, whereas the family child engaged in parent's business got considerable time to play and be off from work. It was also noticed that apart from consanguinity, communal affinity also played a part in getting sympathetic treatment. Any way, it cannot be denied that child mind is ingenious and it devises means of diversion from work and g e in play or pleasures of liberty. Let us however, look at Table 4 which speaks about the availability of leisure to child labour in the silk industry of Bhagalpur, which has been prepared on the basis of answers received to our question on work and leisure.

Evidently, the Table 4(a) shows that of the 250 respondents 22.40 percent said that they work continuously and do not have rest intervals. But 74% affirmed that they enjoyed daily leisure. Only a small number of 3.60% of respondents did not reply to the question.

Such a situation prompted another question by the investigator. Those who enjoyed leisure regularly were 185 people (out of 250 respondents). It was in regard to the leisure hour. In reply 45.41 percent held out that they got a leisure of 30 mts. daily during working hours; 12.97 percent came out with the reply that they get 60 mts. respite whereas 41.62% affirmed that at best they get 45 mts. rest intervals.

Next question obviously related to weekly rest. Replies elicited from respondents are given below in Table 4 (b).

We get the following picture from the above table. 12.40% respondents confirmed that Sunday is their weekly rest day. 87.60% said that they take Friday as their weekly off day. Evidently they are Muslim child labour. What is interesting here to note is that off days on Sunday or Friday depend upon the liking of the child labour. If he wants to work on these days, he can, in order to earn regular wages. It is not a compulsory sabbath, but optional rest day.

Midday meal, breakfast or tea is also a vital point to be looked into. As such the child labour respondents were asked to clarify if they get meal, breakfast or tea during lunch hour

TABLE 4

Working Children and Their Leisure Hour

Age Group	*Type of Response*							
	Yes		*No*		*N.R.*		*Total*	
	N.	*P.*	*N.*	*P.*	*N.*	*P.*	*N.*	*P.*
5—7	6	66.67	1	11.11	2	22.22	9	100.00
8—10	38	73.08	13	25.00	1	1.92	52	100.00
11—13	98	74.24	29	21.97	5	3.79	132	100.00
Upto 14	43	75.44	13	22.81	1	1.76	57	100.00
Total	185	74.00	56	22.40	9	3.60	250	100.00

TABLE 4 (a)

Duration of Leisure

Age Group	*Duration*							
	30 minutes		*45 minutes*		*1 hour*		*Total*	
	N.	*P.*	*N.*	*P.*	*N.*	*P.*	*N.*	*P.*
5—7	1	16.67	3	50.00	2	33.33	6	100.00
8—10	7	18.42	27	71.05	4	10.53	38	100.00
11—13	53	54.08	33	33.67	12	12.25	98	100.00
Upto 14	23	53.49	14	32.56	6	13.95	43	100.00
Total	84	45.41	77	41.62	24	12.97	185	100.00

TABLE 4 (b)

Days	*Rest Day* *N.*	*P.*
Sunday	31	12.40
Friday	219	87.60
Total	250	100.00

from the employer ? Replies obtained from them are put in Table 4 (c).

It was pleasant to note that 65.60% of respondents confirmed supply of breakfast or tea during lunch hour. 4.40% did not express themselves either in favour of or against any such provision. Thirty percent respondents informed that they did not get any meal, breakfast or tea from their employer.

Now even these figures had a special bearing on the community bondage, personal relation or some humanitarian approach between the employer and the employees. Of the 65.60% respondents out of 250 persons interviewed which comes to about 164 people a question was aimed as to what do they get as supplementary diet during duty hours. Data collected on this account are shown in Table 4 (c) (i).

The data reveal that out of 65.60% only 4.88% respondents get daily breakfast during duty hours. They were found to be relatives of the employer, or belonging to their caste or religious groups and were possibly neighbours also. 9.76% related that they get breakfast of some sort only, say fried rice etc. But the vast majority of 80.48 percent respondents confirmed that they got only tea during duty hours from their employers. But they also reported that it does not come to them daily, it comes when the master so wills. The remaining 4.88% also confirmed that they are supplied with tea or poor breakfast like Sattu, Grams or fried rice irregularly, once or twice in a week.

Wages

It is a world phenomenon that children are paid low wages.

TABLE 4 (c)

Respondents Opinion on Whether They Get Any Meal from Their Employer or Not

Religion	*Type of Response*							
	Yes		*No*		*N. R.*		*Total*	
	N.	*P.*	*N.*	*P.*	*N.*	*P.*	*N.*	*P.*
Hindu	18	31.13	26	56.52	2	4.35	46	100.00
Muslim	146	71.57	49	24.02	9	4.41	204	100.00
Total	164	65.60	75	30.00	11	4.40	250	100.00

TABLE 4 (c) (i)

Religion	Specification									
	Breakfast		Meal		Tea		Any other		Total	
	N.	P.	N.	P.	N.	P.	N.	P.	N.	P.
Hindu	2	11.11	—	—	15	83.33	1	5.56	18	100.00
Muslim	14	9.59	8	5.48	117	80.14	7	4.79	146	100.00
Total	16	9.76	8	4.88	132	80.48	8	4.88	164	100.00

Bhagalpur Silk Industry is no exception. Coming from economically distressed people's families, these children engaged in silk industry of Bhagalpur are content to get what they receive. They have no voice to record their protest, none such philanthropic spokesman who can advocate the child labour's cause, nor do the children have any union, or are sponsored by any union who could ultimately raise their voice against child-labour exploitation. What is surprising is the sight that a boy of 16 or 17 years of age may be doing the same job and may draw Rs. 15/- to Rs. 16/- per day, whereas the lad below 14 years may get just Rs. 5/- or Rs. 6/- per diem. As such the destitute is destined to remain a destitute even though he labours hard to win his bread. Labour and wages are never commensurate with each other in the case of children employed in private industries. Perhaps the situation of labour begetting penury would arouse a Marx from his grave and once again lead an international struggle for improving children's lot. The following data as the Table 5 reveals might convince every awakened soul about the necessity for raising children's wages problems in international forum.

The data present a figure of 37.20 percent who admitted that they get only Rs. 5/- per day. 49.20% respondents confessed that they get Rs. 6/- to Rs. 10/- per day. But 13.60% respondents confirmed that they get Rs. 15/- per day, a very lucrative payment when considered in the light of lowest wages paid to 37.20 percent respondents. Wages are adequate or inadequate only in relation to market prices of essential commodities. If it is a case of price-hike, wages such as these mentioned herein are definitely low and need to be restructured. It is indeed a fruit of ignorance that while children are not covered by Minimum Wages Act, they continue to work and be exploited without any hope of resurrection.

The method of payment, daily, weekly or monthly is also a matter of concern for those who enquire into the prevailing conditions of child labour from economic point of view. In

TABLE 5

Child Labour and Their Wages

Variable	*Wages*							
	Upto Rs. 5/-		*Rs. 6/-to 10/-*		*Rs. 11/- to 15/-*		*Total*	
	N.	*P.*	*N.*	*P.*	*N.*	*P.*	*N.*	*P.*
5—7	9	100.00	—	—	—	—	9	100.00
8—10	31	59.62	19	36.54	2	3.84	52	100.00
11—13	46	34.85	77	55.33	9	6.82	132	100.00
Upto 14	7	12.28	27	47.37	23	40.25	57	100.00
Total	93	37.20	123	40.20	34	13.60	250	100.00

fact, all the three systems prevail, but what catches investigator's eyes is the unwritten process of restraining a part amount of wages due in order to keep it as security money. It is like a rope round the waist of the child labour bound to the job they perform. Child labour cannot be a run-away if his money is kept in the custody of the employer. To study this aspect of payment of wages to children employed in silk industry of Bhagalpur data were obtained through answers to certain questions put to them. The data are put up in Table 6.

Nearly 70% respondents gave out that they are paid their remuneration weekly. 12.40 percent of the respondents receive their wages monthly. Rest 17.60% draw their wages daily. Behind such payments, restraining part of wages from making over full amount to earners was as conspicuous as payment itself, yet there was no protest nor even a murmur on this account.

The researcher felt it necessary now to explore from the respondents if they considered their wages satisfactory. Questions to this effect were put to the respondents. Replies received have been classified according to age, education and general income as variable and these have been placed in statistical form in Table 7.

Data collected show results as : 24.40 percent out of the total sample opined in favour by telling that they were satisfied with their wages, but a large majority of 73.60 percent belonging to different age-group expressed adversely that they were not satisfied with their wages. The respondents who expressed satisfaction belonged to the age-group of 8 to 14 years which is indeed a period of immaturity. Data collected on the basis of the variable of education revealed that illiterates 16.42 percent and literate upto Primary standard 26.11 percent felt satisfied with their wages. This was due to compulsion of circumstances, because illiterates would not be able to find diverse and richer avenues of earning. Even children having read up to Middle standard (34.62%) had the same fate and no occupational

TABLE 6

Variable	Wages period							
	Daily		*Weekly*		*Monthly*		*Total*	
Age Group	*N.*	*P.*	*N.*	*P.*	*N.*	*P.*	*N.*	*P.*
5—7	2	22.22	6	66.67	1	11.11	9	100.00
8 - 10	8	15.38	41	78.85	3	5.77	52	100.00
11—13	23	17.42	104	78.79	5	3.79	132	100.00
Upto 14	11	19.30	24	42.11	22	38.59	57	100 00
Total	44	17.60	175	70.00	31	12.40	250	100.00

TABLE 7

Respondent's Opinion on Whether They are Satisfied with Their Wages or Not

Variables	*Type of Response*							
	Yes		*No*		*N.R.*		*Total*	
	N.	*P.*	*N.*	*P.*	*N.*	*P.*	*N.*	*P.*
Age-Group								
5-7	2	22.22	6	66.67	1	11.11	9	100.00
8—10	7	13.46	44	84.62	1	1.92	52	100 00
11—13	26	19.70	103	78.03	3	2.27	132	100.00
Upto 14	26	45.61	31	54.39	—	—	57	100.00
Total	61	24.40	184	73.60	5	2.00	250	100.00
Education								
Illiterate	11	16.42	54	80.60	2	2.98	67	100.00
Primary	41	26.11	114	72.61	2	1.28	157	100.00
Middle	9	34.62	16	61.54	1	3.84	26	100.00
Total	61	24.40	184	73.60	5	2.00	250	100.00

Income (Yearly in Rupees)							
Upto 5000/-	3	3.26	87	94.57	2	2.17	92
50001—10000/-	24	20.69	90	77.59	2	1.12	116
10001—15000/-	21	75.00	6	21.43	1	3.57	28
15001 and above	13	92.85	1	7.15	—	—	14
Total	61	24.40	184	73.60	5	2.00	250

choice but to rest content with what they had. But a great majority of 61.54% respondents read up to Middle standard emphatically expressed their dissatisfaction with their wages. Only 3.84% middle standard trained respondents had nothing to say : they believe silence is golden when no change is possible. To sum up, therefore, out of 250 respondents 61 persons constituting 24.40% expressed satisfaction; 184 persons out of 250 making 73.60% expressed dissatisfaction and 5 persons equal to 2% had nothing to say. These figures speak for respondents on the basis of Education Variables.

The next variable that concerned the researcher was Income basis, and this too was studied empirically. It transpired that respondents getting up to Rs. 5000/- (Five thousand annually) were the disgruntled lot whose figures stood at 94.57% i.e., 87 out of 92 persons in this income category. The satisfied respondents constituted 3.26% i.e., 3 out of 92 persons and 2.17% had nothing to say on the subject.

In the income group of 5001/- to Rs. 10,000/- the figures stood at 20.69% satisfied, 77.59% dissatisfied and 1.72% had nothing to say out of 116 respondents.

In the higher income group of Rs. 10,001/- to Rs. 15000/- the number of respondents satisfied with their wages was 75% and 21.43% dissatisfied, and finally 3.57% respondents kept silent on the query. The respondents who came in this group were only 28.

Finally in the highest family income group of the sample that is drawing between Rs. 15,001/- and above, 92.85% stood in the column of satisfied people, and 7.15% dissatisfied. The respondents totalled only 14 in this highest family income group.

We can, therefore, observe that the lower the family income, the higher the number of dissatisfied people, and the higher the family income, the lower the number of dissatisfied respondents. This is only natural for wage earners, because with increased wages go their increased amenities of life and increased pleasures. But what is sad that this Table reveals is the fact that out of 250 respondents, people belonging to lowest family income group were 92, (in the family annual income strata of Rs. 5000/-) and 116 in the annual family income of Rs. 5001/- to Rs. 10,000/-. Persons in the higher annual family income were only 28 and in the highest group were only 14. Thus these figures speak that on the whole child labour working in the silk industry of Bhagalpur mostly came from low family income group, and they do so because the necessity of augmenting family income in order to save members from starvation, stand acute and demand immediate remedy. The child is the only wealth with such parents, which can be pawned to save members from extinction.

The researcher felt justified in exploring as to how the child labour engaged in the silk industry of Bhagalpur utilises its earning. During field investigation and direct interview it transpired that they spend the money towards augmenting their family's income, thus providing greater economic assistance to their family. It also came to the investigator's notice that some children keep their wages as their personal money and utilise their earning towards their personal needs or pleasures. Yet, quite a good number of them expressed that they join silk production to learn techniques and skill so that they will begin their own trade when they have accumulated both money and training. Table 8 speaks clearly on these points.

Statements

(a) Give to their parents,

(b) Keep a part with himself,

(c) Deposit in Bank or Post Office,

(d) Entirely spend on himself.

TABLE 8

Utilization of Wages

Variable	*a.* N.	*a.* P.	*b.* N.	*b.* P.	*c.* N.	*c.* P.	*d.* N.	*d.* P.	*Total* N.	*Total* P.
Age-Group										
5—7	9	100.00	—	—	—	—	—	—	9	100.00
8—10	48	92.31	4	7.69	—	—	—	—	52	100.00
11—13	67	50.76	26	19.70	38	28.79	1	0.75	132	100.00
Upto 14	25	43.86	9	15.79	16	28.07	7	12.28	57	100.00
Total	149	59.60	39	15.60	54	21.60	8	3.20	250	100.00

It is revealed in regards to the question as to how they utilise their money that 59.60 percent of the respondents make over their earning to their parents for family assistance, whereas 3.20 percent keep their money with themselves and spend on themselves. However 21.60% stated that they deposit their earnings in Banks or Post Offices. 15.60% respondents said that they keep a part of their wages as savings in Banks and the rest amount they pass on to their parents for family expenses.

After money matters, spending leisure time is also a matter of interest. We have already mentioned that a weekly off day on Sunday or Friday is either a day of play or rest or additional work to earn added livelihood. It all depends on the choice of the child labour. As such, a question was put to the respondents. How do they spend their leisure day ? Data collected are given in Table 9.

Figures in Table 9 reveal that a large majority of 68.80% respondents spend their off day in games and plays. A minority group of respondents, viz, 7.20 percent stated that they take rest in their homes. The residual percentage of 24.00 maintained that they assist their parents in domestic duties, cleaning home or the ground attached to their homes or their fields if any. Data have been collected considering the age-group as an important factor that influences their manner of spending their off days. The bigger the boy, the greater his preoccupation both in home or outside.

Painful is the song of the working child in developing countries. The same holds true about Indian child at work, and those employed in Bhagalpur silk industry are just a part of the class. The working child seems everywhere in misery and in chains. The researcher felt curious to ascertain if the children engaged in silk industry of Bhagalpur are satisfied with their jobs or not; if not, why ? Therefore, to be more rationalistic care was taken while collecting data to classify respondents according to age-group, educational standard and income status

TABLE 9

Respondent's Routine During Holidays

Variable	*Response*							
	Rest		*Helping Parents at home/field*		*Simply play*		*Total*	
	N.	*P.*	*N.*	*P.*	*N.*	*P.*	*N.*	*P.*
Age-Group								
5—7	—	—	—	—	9	100.00	9	100.00
8—10	9	17.31	11	21.15	32	61.54	52	100.00
11—13	2	1.52	13	9.85	117	88.63	132	100.00
Upto 14	7	12.28	36	63.16	14	24.56	57	100.00
Total	18	7.20	60	24.00	172	68.80	250	100.00

which were the essential variables. All these are reflected in Table 10.

From the figures it transpires that according to age-group variable, 74.70 percent respondents, constituting the largest majority expressed dissatisfaction with their jobs because there is nothing like going up the ladder, meaning promotions or time bound scale for increments. Over and above their remuneration was pitiably low, inadequate to meet daily needs during present price-rise. The job itself is sedantry and causing various maladies of skin, lungs and stomach.

But there are some who are always reconciled to fate and circumstances. 23.60 percent respondents were of the view that the job is their luck and they are satisfied. They attributed their taste and their skill suitable for their jobs. Data as collected with education and income as variables are presented in the break-up scheme under Table 10.

Such informations naturally led the researcher to enquire if the respondents would shift to another job should such an opportunity come their way. They said such a change in profession, especially when it would be lucrative, would be most welcome. Data placed in Table 11 are worthy of close consideration.

Figures arrived at reveal that 88.40% of the respondents were in favour of change in jobs if favourable opportunity came before them. Something like 10% of the respondents did not show an inclination for changing jobs. A miniscule proportion of 1.60% did not reply in clear terms. It was as if they abstained from the enquiry which was only natural because they were quite young, immature and unenlightened.

But when description of alternative jobs was enquired into the respondents were unambiguous though of varied taste. Their replies are collected in Table 11 A.

TABLE 10

Respondent's Views on Satisfaction with Job

Variable	*Types of Response*							
	Yes		*No*		*N.R.*		*Total*	
	N.	*P.*	*N.*	*P.*	*N.*	*P.*	*N.*	*P.*
Age-Group								
5—7	1	11.11	7	77.78	1	11.11	9	100.00
8—10	13	25.00	38	73.08	1	1.92	52	100.00
11—13	26	19.70	104	78.79	2	1.51	132	100.00
Upto 14	19	33.33	38	66.67	—	—	57	100.00
Total	59	23.60	187	74.80	4	1.60	250	100.00
Education								
Illiterate	24	35.82	41	61.19	2	2.99	67	10.000
Primary	26	16.56	129	82.17	2	1.27	157	100.00
Middle	9	34.61	17	65.39	—	—	26	100.00
Total	59	23 60	187	74.80	4	1.60	250	100.00

Income (Yearly in Rupees)								
Upto 5000/-	11	11.96	79	85.87	2	2.11	92	100.00
5001-10,000	17	14.66	97	83.62	2	1.72	116	100.00
10,001 15,000	19	67.86	9	32.14	—	—	28	100.00
15,001 & above	12	85.71	2	14.29	—	—	14	100.00
Total	59	23.60	187	74.80	4	1.60	250	100.00

TABLE 11

Respondent's Views on Acceptance of Another Work

Variabie	*Type of Response*							
	Yes		*No*		*N.R.*		*Total*	
	N.	*P.*	*N.*	*P.*	*N.*	*P.*	*N.*	*P.*
Age-Group								
5—7	7	77.78	1	11.11	1	11.11	9	100.00
8—10	42	80.77	8	15.38	2	3.85	52	100.00
11—13	118	89.39	12	9.85	1	0.76	132	100.00
Upto 14	54	93.74	3	6.26	—	—	57	100.00
Total	221	88.40	25	10.00	4	1.60	250	100.00

Quite a number of respondents sought jobs related to weaving, some preferred its mechanical side, say repairs of powerlooms, other wanted to join other spheres of trade not related to weaving silk. Data reveal that only 37.56% respondents expressed liking for mechanical side of maintaining powerloom. The majority of respondents comprising 62.44%, wanted completely different trades. 28.96% among them wanted to quit weaving jobs and enter schools for gradual enlightenment. Some of them preferred to do domestic jobs as servants who made 4.98%, some liked labourer's job, that is 4.98%, mechanical works were liked by 7.24, Drivers, Cleaners jobs were to the taste of 4.50% and Electrician's jobs were chosen by 9.50%. Other minor works were liked by 2.26% of child respondents. This valuable information is elicited from Table 11 A.

Insecurity in jobs looms large before the child labour involved in Bhagalpur silk industry. Most of them are temporary employees and the whim of the employer counts supreme. As such each hired child and his parents try to keep the master or employer in good humour so that no harm can be done to the child. Retrenchment, dismissal or even temporary removal from service will mean an unkind cut to the employee's shattered economy. In such circumstances of penury the question of developing child's personality, instilling in them great cultural qualities or cherishing high aspiration do not arise either in the parents or in the child. Insecurity and fear of future keep the child labour in eternal bondage.

Questions in this regard were put to the child respondents and the facts are seen in Table 12.

From the Table 12, it is studied that 62.40 percent respondents made a clean breast of their insecurity in the silk industry of Bhagalpur. Only 7.20% proclaimed that there was no such anxiety on account of insecurity, or in other words, they felt they were secure in their jobs. But fear gripped at least 26% respondents and they kept their feelings restrained by

TABLE 11A

Respondent's Preference to Work

Variable	*Type of Response*					
	a.		*b.*		*c.*	
	N.	*P.*	*N.*	*P.*	*N.*	*P.*
1	2	3	4	5	6	7
Age-Group						
5—7	4	51.29	1	14.29	1	14.29
8—10	15	35.71	1	2.38	3	7.17
11—13	37	31.36	7	5.93	3	2.54
Upto 14	8	14.82	2	3.70	4	7.41
Total	64	28.96	11	4.98	11	4.92

(*Contd.*)

d.		e.		f.		g.		h.		Total	
N.	P.	N.	P.	N.	P.	N.	P.	N.	P.	N.	P.
8	9	10	11	12	13	14	15	16	17	18	19
—	—	—	—	1	14.29	—	—	—	—	7	100.00
4	9.53	2	4.76	12	28.58	3	7.14	2	4.76	42	100.00
9	7.63	6	5.08	43	36.45	11	9.32	2	1.69	118	100.00
3	5.56	2	3.70	27	50.00	7	12.96	1	1.85	54	100.00
16	7.24	10	4.52	83	37.56	21	7.50	5	2.26	221	100.00

N.B. : Detail of work :

a. Enter a school for study
b. Work as a domestic servant
c. Works as a farm labourer
d. Learn Mechanical work,
e. Driver, cleaner
f. Loom mechanic
g. Electrician
h. Any other.

TABLE 12

Respondent's Views on Job Security

Variable	*Type of Response*									
	Yes		*No*		*Can't say*		*N.R.*		*Total*	
	N.	*P.*	*N.*	*P.*	*N.*	*P.*	*N.*	*P.*	*N.*	*P.*
Age										
5-7	1	11.11	1	11.11	4	44.45	3	33.33	9	100.00
8—10	22	42.31	4	7.69	21	40.38	5	9.62	52	100.00
11—13	89	67.42	6	4.55	36	27.37	1	0.76	132	100.00
Upto 14	44	77.19	7	12.28	4	7.02	2	3-51	57	100.00
Total	156	62.40	18	7.20	65	26.00	11	4.40	250	100.00

Education										
Illiterate	19	28.36	4	5.97	37	55.22	7	10.45	67	100.00
Primary	123	78.34	6	3.82	24	15.29	4	2.55	157	100.00
Middle	14	53.85	8	30.77	4	15.38	—	—	26	100.00
Total	156	62.40	18	7.20	65	26.00	11	4.40	250	100.00

telling 'cant say'. 4.40 percent of respondents were still more clever. They did not welcome the question, nor offered any reply.

On the basis of education variables, the same pattern of reply emerges. A great majority of 78.34% respondents having primary education replied that they feel insecurity, since no guarantee of jobs is given to them. Even the respondents having Middle standard education comprising about 53.85% expressed themselves as insecure along with 28.36% illiterates. Respondents who stated that they felt secure comprised 5.97% illiterates, primary trained 3.82% and Middle trained 30.77%.

Type of employment naturally evoked another question. Whether the child labour involved in Bhagalpur silk indurtry were casual, temporary or permanent employees is a pertinent question that follows as a consequence of the informations given in Table 12. The respondents were quick to offer their replies to the question : "Is your job casual/temporary/or permanent ? Data are reflected in Table 13.

The figures obtained above reflect that a vast majority of 61.20% of respondents were casual employees while only 38% were classified as temporary, only 0.80% percent were permanent in their jobs. Other details based on age and education variables are clearly placed in Table 13.

During field investigation the researcher felt inclined to ask three questions from the respondents just to record their perception towards their place in the family. The questions were in the form of statements and the respondents were asked to express their agreement or disagreement with the statements. The first statement put up for their answer was : Working boys/girls received good attention from their parents. Second statement was : A working boy/girl develops self-confidence, and third was : A working boy/girl becomes economically independent.

TABLE 13

Nature of Job

Variable	Type of Response							
	Casual		Temporary		Permanent		Total	
	N.	P.	N.	P.	N.	P.	N.	P.
1	2	3	4	5	6	7	8	9
Age								
5—7	6	66.67	3	33.33	—	—	9	100.00
8—10	39	75.00	13	25.00	—	—	52	100.00
11—13	91	68.94	41	31.06	—	—	132	100.00
Upto 14	17	29.82	38	66.67	2	3.51	57	100.00
Total	153	61.20	95	38.00	2	0.20	250	100.00

(*Contd.*)

1	2	3	4	5	6	7	8	9
Education								
Illiterate	44	65.67	23	34.33	—	—	67	100.00
Primary	102	64.97	55	35.03	—	—	157	100.00
Middle	7	26.92	17	65.39	2	7.69	26	100.00
Total	153	61.20	95	38.00	2	0.20	250	100.00

Replies were elicited quickly and without hesitation. Data produced in this regard are placed in Table 14.

The informations may be summarised as under: 87.60 percent respondents stated that it is true, a working boy/girl receives good attention from parents, while 12.40 percent of them expressed disagreement with this view.

The second statement was met with 52.40% respondents agreeing with it, while 47.60 respondents disagreed with the view that a child develops self confidence while he works.

Data in regards to the third statement show that only 17.20% agreed with the statement that a working boy/girl becomes economically independent. Yet a great majority of 82.80% respondents disagreed with the statement, the reason being that they live in family sharing each other's pleasure and pain and also economic gains.

A peep into the private lives of the child respondents becomes necessary when we have studied their economic life in all its dimensions. We have observed their responses to the question as to how do they utilise their wages. Pocket money may be used both worthily or unworthily. Urbanity has its own good and bad effects on child mind. The process of socialization is often invisible, yet it is always there. With all the vast attempt at publicity regarding Cigarettes, drinks and other luxuries available with money, the child mind is easily impressed and fascinated. It is difficult to escape the baneful effects of such propaganda of smoking and drinks. Therefore it seemed pertinent to ask the child labour (relating to Bhagalpur silk industry) if they had the habit of smoking or drinking ? Of course, it was difficult to draw out truthful responses, either to their shyness, fear of being caught, social degradation or such like stigma, yet they could be coaxed to give themselves out, when they were assured of full safely. Their responses are placed in Table 15.

TABLE 14

Respondent's Opinion Towards Some Statements

Variable	*Agree*		*Disagree*		*Total*	
	N.	*P.*	*N.*	*P.*	*N.*	*P.*
1	2	3	4	5	6	7
			A			
Age						
5—7	7	77.18	2	22.22	9	100.00
8—10	46	88.46	6	11.54	52	100.00
11—13	113	85.61	19	14.39	132	100.00
Upto 14	53	92.98	4	7.02	57	100.00
Total	219	87.60	31	12.40	250	100.00

(Contd.)

B.						C.					
Agree		Disagree		Total		Agree		Disagree		Total	
N.	P.	N.	P.	N.	P.	N.	P.	N.	P.	N.	P.
8	9	10	11	12	13	14	15	16	17	18	19
5	55.56	4	44.44	9	100.00	3	33.33	6	66.67	9	100.00
21	40.38	31	59.62	52	100.00	4	7.69	48	82.31	52	100.00
7	55.30	59	44.70	132	100.00	25	18.94	107	81.06	132	100.00
32	56.14	25	43.86	57	100.00	11	19.30	46	80.70	57	100.00
131	52.40	119	47.60	250	100.00	43	17.20	207	82.80	250	100.00

A. A working boy/girl receive good attention of parents.

B. A working boy/girl develops self confidence.

C. A working boy/girl becomes economically independent.

TABLE 15

Respondent's Habits

Variable	*Type of Response*							
	Yes		*No*		*N.R.*		*Total*	
	N.	*P.*	*N.*	*P.*	*N.*	*P.*	*N.*	*P.*
Age								
5—7	—	—	8	88.89	1	11.11	9	100.00
8—10	1	1.92	49	94.23	2	3.85	52	100.00
11—13	26	19.70	102	77.27	4	3.03	132	100.00
Up to 14	17	29.82	39	68.43	1	1.75	57	100.00
Total	44	17.60	198	79.20	8	3.20	250	100.00

Education								
Illiterate	9	13.43	55	82.09	3	4.48	67	100.00
Primary	24	15.29	128	81.53	5	3.18	157	100.00
Middle	11	42.31	15	57.69	—	—	26	100.00
Total	44	17.60	198	79.20	8	3.20	250	100.00

Data brought out in the Table show 79.20 percent respondents free from any evil habits of smoking, drinking or chewing tobacco. Of course, 17.60% confessed their bad habits. 3.20 percent of respondents did not reply. Children addicted to smoking etc., belong to the age group of 14 years and educated upto Middle standard. At least 29.82% addicts belong to the age group of 14 years and 42.31% are those who are literate upto Middle standard. More details are offered in the Table 15 itself.

Consequently, further probe was felt necessary. It would be profitable to know their choice of the material of addiction. A question was, therefore, put to those respondents who had confessed their use of smoking/drinks/chewing etc. Data obtained on this account are placed in Table 15 A.

Surprisingly, 52.27% of them narrated that they take tobacco is one form or another, while only 9.07% said that they tasted alcohol. Rest of them, 38.64% gave out that they smoke Biri or Cigarette. Painfully enough, there is no agency available to help them to desist from bad habits, neither education, nor good counsel.

Articles of luxury are a dream for everyone. Even children are not devoid of such desires. The child who labours for wages too wishes to have good clothes, a cycle, good food, and if he is more urbanised he seeks to have a T.V., a Transistor or a Tape recorder. Desires multiply and they are infectious too. If Mr. A purchases a transistor, Mr. B would fix his ambition to possess a T.V. The child on the Powerloom drevms to have a cycle or a transistor to keep away his drudgery. The researcher has delved deep into this tender aspect of a child mind which she has placed in Table 16.

Figures obtained and given above reflect clearly the aspirations of the respondents, viz, 31.20% want to buy good clothes; 8.80% want transistors, 27.60 percent dream of Television sets. A good number of 17.60 percent respondents desire for wrist

TABLE 15A

Specification of Habits

Variable	*Biri smoking*		*Tobacco*		*Alcohal*		*Total*	
	N.	*P.*	*N.*	*P.*	*N.*	*P.*	*N.*	*P.*
1	2	3	4	5	6	7	8	9
Age								
5—7	—	—	—	—	—	—	—	
8—10	—	—	1	100.00	—	—	1	100.00
11—13	11	42.31	14	53.85	1	3.84	26	100.00
Upto 14	6	35.29	8	47.06	3	17.65	17	100.00
Total	17	30.64	23	52.27	4	9.00	44	100.00

(*Contd.*)

1	2	3	4	5	6	7	8	9
Education								
Illiterate	3	33.33	5	55.56	1	11.11	9	100.00
Primary	10	41.67	13	54.17	1	4.16	24	100.00
Middle	4	36.36	5	45.46	2	18.18	11	100.00
Total	17	38.64	23	52.27	4	9.09	44	100.00

TABLE 16

Respondent's Opinion on what they would like to Purchase from their Earning

Variable	*Like to Purchase*											
	Cycle		*Watch*		*Good clothes*		*Transistor*		*T.V*		*Total*	
	N.	*P.*	*N.*	*P.*	*N.*	*P.*	*N.*	*P.*	*N.*	*P.*	*N.*	*P.*
1	2	3	4	5	6	7	8	9	10	11	12	13
Age												
5—7	1	11.11	1	11.11	2	22.22	1	11.11	4	44.48	9	100.00
8—10	4	7.69	13	25.00	12	23.08	3	5.77	20	38.46	52	100.00
11—13	26	19.70	19	14.39	47	35.61	13	9.85	27	20.45	132	100.00
Upto 14	6	10.53	11	19.30	17	29.82	5	8.77	18	31.58	57	100.00
Total	37	14.80	44	17.60	78	31.20	22	8.80	69	27.60	250	100.00

(*Contd.*)

1	2	3	4	5	6	7	8	9	10	11	12	13
Education												
Illiterate	13	19.40	11	16.42	25	37.31	4	5.97	14	20.90	67	100.00
Primary	19	12.10	29	18.47	46	29.30	17	10.83	46	29.30	157	100.00
Middle	5	19.23	4	15.38	7	26.92	1	3.85	9	34.62	26	100.00
Total	37	14.80	44	17.60	78	31.20	22	8.80	69	27.60	250	10.000

watches, and the rest 14.80 percent of them think of acquiring bicycles.

Finally, before the researcher wanted to close her field investigation she wanted to know the child's and his parent's awareness of legal protective measures promulgated from time to time. Jurists and social workers, philanthropists and legislators witnessed the said state of affairs encircling the destitute, the famished or the economically down-trodden child whose destiny it was 'to labour and to wait.' If such childs' labour had corrected and improved family well-being and relieved them from economic distress, much would have been achieved. But the spectacle remains gloomy even inspite of child' labour. It was more a tale of a child sacrificing his childhood, and adults watching how he is growing anaemic both in body and in mind. It was difficult, may, impossible to overlook the slow wastage of the pillars of future, the coming generation that would lead the nation : Bhagalpur silk industry and the child working therein were just a part and parcel of the agonising spectacle that obtain in the developing world. As such the researcher wanted to close her work after going through the aspect of people's awareness of the present day laws on child labour. The informations are placed in Table 17. Questions were put to parents first.

Data collected speak volumes. Among the fathers (of the child labourer) 8.40 percent said that they had heard of some protective laws meant for safeguarding children and only 0.40 percent mothers (of the child labourers) confessed in favour of legislative processes meant for saving child from cruel exploitation. Others, that is, the parents of those children who were working as labourers completely drew a blank. They had no knowledge of government rules protecting children and their figure was enormous that is about 88.80 percent.

Consequently, another question percolated towards the respondents who were the parents of the working child, and who confirmed in the earlier interrogation their awareness of certain

TABLE 17

Respondent, and Their Parents Awareness to the Laws Made for Child Labour

Respondent and their Parents	*Type of Response*							
	Yes		*No*		*N. R.*		*Total*	
	N.	*P.*	*N.*	*P.*	*N.*	*P.*	*N.*	*P.*
Respondent	1	0.40	238	95.20	11	4.40	250	100.00
Father	21	8.40	222	88.80	7	2.80	250	100.00
Mother	1	0.40	245	98.00	4	1.60	250	100.00
Total	23	3.87	705	94.00	22	2.93	750	100.00

legislations issued in favour of children. The results are put forth in Table 18.

Such parents who had knowledge of the Children Act were a few in number. 80.95 percent of Father respondents (number 21), said that the present laws are sufficient for protecting the working child provided they are sincerely implemented. On the mother side, only one came forward to state that she too had some information about such beneficial measures. On being asked about their source of information, the fathers claimed that they were members of trade unions, as such facts were always discussed in their group meetings. Also, they gathered information from Radio and Television media that always and quite regularly published democratic measures concerning public welfare. The single mother said that her husband had communicated to her these ideas which she was pleased to remember.

To conclude, the researcher flings the last question at the respondents and their parents. Would they suggest any new laws to ameliorate the working child's conditions, his safety, his growing up as a full human being ? The child had nothing to say, but the parents blinked for a while, then mustered strength to make some suggestions, vague and circumbulatory, yet they could mumble a bit which is produced in Table 19.

Evidently, only 0.80 percent of the father suggested that while the existing laws are quite good, more care should be given to children up to 14 years of age, so that their growth is not inhibited. While laws of the country forbade employment of children up to 14 years in any workhouse, yet poverty compelled them to put their children in factories and other industries so that they may be able to drive the wolf from the door. Since Bhagalpur has predominantly only one industry, that is silk industry, parents are bound to take advantage of the manufacturing houses where their children can earn and learn simultaneously.

To round up the whole investigation programme, we can say that we have visualised the entire problem of the child

TABLE 18

Respondents and Their Parents Evaluation of Such Laws

Respondent and their Parents	*Type of Response*									
	Yes		*No*		*Can't say*		*N.R.*		*Total*	
	N.	*P.*	*N.*	*P.*	*N.*	*P.*	*N.*	*P.*	*N.*	*P.*
Respondent	—	—	1	100.00	—	—	—	—	1	100.00
Father	17	80.95	4	9.05	—	—	—	—	21	100.00
Mother	1	100.00	—	—	—	—	—	—	1	100.00
Total	18	78.26	5	21.74	—	—	—	—	1	100.00

TABLE 19

Respondents Opinion About Any New Law to be Enacted

Respondent and their Parents	*Type of Response*							
	Yes		*No.*		*N.R.*		*Total*	
	N.	*P.*	*N.*	*P.*	*N.*	*P.*	*N.*	*P.*
Respondent	—	—	212	48.80	38	15.20	250	100.00
Father	2	0.30	233	93.20	15	6.00	250	100.00
Mother	—	—	193	77.20	57	22.80	250	100.00
Total	2	0.27	638	85.07	110	14.66	750	100.00

labour in the silk industry of Bhagalpur. The paradigm that we have looked into are essentially human—we have examined the conditions under which children labour in the silk industry, their suitability and adaptability to the job, hires, wages, education, age-group, income status, health and recreation, leisure, utility of money earned, quality of jobs, casual, temporary or permanent, etc. We have also looked into the fact that urbanisation has been influencing them both ways, some good and some bad. We have also taken to account their social awareness of legal measures, viz, the Children Acts and have also drawn them into discussion to suggest more ways and means and enactments to improve the working child's lot. All said and done, the investigation has been fruitful and it leads to certain awakening of the mass-mind to be more human, sympathetic to the working child. A working child below the age of 14 years is not our pride, but slur our nation, yet it can be cherished with the hope that these children will subsequently improve the silk industry of Bhagalpur.

CHAPTER VII

Legal Measures and People's Awareness

Law is like a railway engine sleeping in the Locomotive yard which begins to heave when fuelled and fired. Law will not work until invoked or provoked. This is true, at least, in the case of children for whom all laws are dormant and inoperative against their exploitation. Observers report that there is hardly a case in Indian Courts against employment of children in hazardous jobs. There is actually no prosecution of employers in whose establishment, tiny tots and kids are becoming warped and perverted. No law reaches these lambs of God for their help. Instead there are numerous laws protecting society against erring children, called delinquents. Only recently some legal enactments have been rushed through the Parliament to save the youngster from the acerbic tongue and flesh-tearing lashes of the demoniac masters.

However, such is not the scene in ancient Indian society. Children could not be deprived of their rights to dignity and love, nor could they be allowed to grow depraved or destitutes. Manusmriti lays down (7.152)

कन्यानाम् सम्प्रदानं च कुमाराणां च रक्षणाम् ॥

Girls are to be offered (in marriage), and therefore must be trained in graceful manner and living and boys must be protected (in order to grow as stalwart defenders of the country). Both boys and girls were to be trained in Ashrams for future life. It seems child slavery was not uncommon among Greeks. Kautilya has given such a passage in his Arthashastra :

म्लेच्छानाम् दोषः प्रजां विक्रेतु घातुं वा । नत्वेवार्यस्य दास भावः

The Mleechas (Greeks) indulge in slave trade, but Aryas do not. Further, Kautilya prescribes punishment to the settler, purchaser and witnesses of child slaves and labour. He is emphatic and quite clear : "The selling or mortgaging by Kinsmen of the life of a Sudra who is not a born slave, *and has not attained majority*, but is an Arya in birth shall be punished with a five or Panas, of a Vaisya, 24 Panas ; of a Kshatriya 36 Panas ; of a Brahmin, 48 Panas. If persons other than the Kinsmen do the same, they shall be liable to the three amercements and capital punishment respectively : purchasers and abettors shall likewise be punished. It is no crime for Mleechas to sell or mortgage the life of their own offspring. But never shall an Arya be subjected to slavery.

'But if in order to tide over family troubles, to find money for fines or Court-decrees, or to recover the (confiscated) household implements, the life of an Arya is mortgaged, they (his Kinsmen) shall as soon as possible redeem his (from bondage) ; and more so if he is a youth or an adult capable of giving help.'[1]

Kautilya was clear on the point that children should not be made to do dishonourable work. It was totally against humanity

1. Shamasartry, Dr. R , *Kautilya's Arthashastra*, Third Book, Chapter XIII, Mysore Printing & Publishing House 1967, p. 208.
उदरदास वर्जमायं प्राणं प्राप्त व्यवहारे शूद्रं विक्रयाधानं नमतः
स्वजनस्य द्वादशयणो दण्डः । वैश्यं छि गुणाः ब्राह्मणां चतुर्गुणः ॥

and was shameful. Therefore he prohibited the sale of children for slavery or undeserved labour.[2]

While we cannot say particularly about the apathy or sympathy of Muslim rulers towards children in India, one thing is certain that the young lads and lesses played a great role in developing their home industries, and thereby developed an unparalleled skill of fingers whether it was a case of weaving, polishing, or cutting diamonds. Likewise, howsomuch we speak against British rule in India, and especially about their brutal manner of siphoning Indian wealth to Britain, yet one admiration is spontaneous when they created an awareness about protecting children from being abused or misused in industries. Most likely this awareness dawned upon them by observing in their own country the growth of slums and poverty and consequently child labour, and their perversions as a product of industrial revolution. It was during the most disturbed times in Indian history, that is from 1850 onwards that legislations related to labour, and also directly or obliquely related to children were brought in vogue by the Directors of the East India Company and later by the British Crown governing India. Smt. Tara Ali Baig has summerised it adequately :

"In the late 19th century the first Legislation to be passed was the Apprentices Act of 1850 and the Female Infanticide Act, 1870, followed by the Indian Majority Act, 1875, the Reformatory Schools Act, 1897, the Vaccination Act, 1880, the Guardianship and Wards Act of 1890, which was then ratified by 14 states. It is under this very Act of 1890 that we continue in 1979 to give children in adoption."

"Two other types of Legislation, one relating to Reformatory Services in 1897 modifying the 1867 Act, and the other to

2. गृहजातः दायागतः लब्धक्रीता नामन्यतमं दास मुनाष्टजषं विवंधुकायं नीचे फर्मणि विदेशे दासी वा सत्रभ)य प्रतिविदित गर्भमेण्यां विक्रयधानं नयतः पूर्वः साहसदाङः क्रेतु श्रोतणां च ॥

Industry, the Factories Act, 1881, were also passed. These related to children who were apprehended for anti-social acts and to child labour. Between that date and 1961—nearly a century later, eight different labour Acts have been passed affecting employment of children, while the Probation and Reformatory Legislation was followed by 12 states and 9 Union Territories. It was the 1919-20 Jails Committee Report which led to correctional reforms in India and reformation efforts towards young offenders."[3]

It is in the second half of the twentieth century that the importance of the child, both in himself and as a citizen of tomorrow has been realised. The child is now in the focus of the world attention and welcome sign reads all along the road for the coming babes in the present decade. As UNICEF prophesies one and a half billion children will be born worldwide in the decade of the 90s and as such "there should be no preoccupation as pressing than protecting the lives and the development of the largest generation of children ever to be entrusted to mankind."[4] The U.N. character and the Universal Declaration of Human Rights with a 54 point series of acceptances declare that a child is entitled to the right to survival, to health, education and care and these are fully endorsed by SAARC countries also. The Heads of the states of SAARC and the UNICEF are pressing hard to hold a submit of International Heads of States in the autunm of 1990 to discuss child welfare including the atrocious child labour problem in its entirety. The UNICEF is wide awake to the slow destruction of child's potentiality due to poverty and lack of essential resources in developing countries. And this is an endless human tragedy encircling our society like a wheel of fire. The time is therefore, ripe to consider a meeting of the heads of states or a special session of the United Nations General Assembly, since

3. Baig, Tara Ali, *Children in India*, *op. cit.*, pp. 262-63.
4 *The Hindustan Times*, Delhi, Seturday 23, 1989, An Article by Rehana Sen, 'Positive Strides'.

"such a meeting might also help to bring children to the centre of political and economic concern."[5] Peace and prosperity of the world lie in a happy and healthy upbringing of children. It is a global premise calling for devoted attention. The proposed summit meeting's theme is bound to centre round 'Today's Children—Tomorrow's World.' Thus we have to put in our political will and all financial and social resources to the task of building up a happy world for the coming child.

Herein comes the need for benevolent and rational and protective laws for children. Of course, there can be no complaint that the people of India have failed their child. Indian Parliament and Assemblies have been formulating laws considering the interest of the children, and also enacting/issuing amendments as fresh informations about child's exploitations by industry owners arrive at their doors. The first human approach to children was seen in the Indian Factories Act of 1881 which provided certain safeties. These were :

1. Children below 7 years were not to be employed in any work,
2. Any child above the age of 7 could not be employed to work in two factories separately on the same day,
3. Their working hours would be from morning to evening only for nine hours a day, and night shift,
4. Four holidays a month and rest intervals must be given to child employees,
5. Dangerous machines must be fenced to save children from being crushed.

However, this Act could be applied where 100 or more workers were employed. Even then there was no official machinery to detect and chase debasement of the provisions, until at last

5. *The State of the World's Children*, 1989, New York, U.S.A. UNICEF's Publication.

in 1891 it was amended and child's working age was raised to 9 years from 7 years, working hours were reduced from 9 to 7 hours. These privileges were extended under Indian Mines Act also. Yet another amendment was made when electric power was introduced in Indian industries. The Factories Act of 1911 reduced children's working hours to six only each day. Age Certificate of each child, as also his physical fitness certificate were made essential.

Better times come to children in 1922 when under the aegis of International Labour Conventions, a factory was said to be a premise; where 20 or more people worked and child was defined to be a person who had not completed 15 years of age. A child would work for 6 hours a day with half an hour's rest in between. Effective official machinery was now introduced for check of irregularities in factory working and imposing penalty in cases of defaults. Amendments came one after another until in 1933 a Children's (Pledging of Labour Act) was enacted by the Government of India on the recommendation of the Royal Commission on Labour. The main aim of this Act was to eliminate the evils arising out of the pledging of the labour of young children by their kinsmen or parents for any monetary consideralion as their benefit. This brings us near Kautilya's pronouncements on child labour earlier referred to. In 1935 this was further improved upon by fixing five hours of labour for a child between 12 and 15 years of age. This was followed by very significant declarations of the Twenty-third Session of the International Labour Conference held in 1937. They adopted a convention in which a special article for India was inserted, fixing the minimum age at which children may be employed or may work in certain occupation. That article reads as follows :

"Children under the age of 13 years shall not be employed or work in the Transport of passengers or goods, or mails, by rail, or in the handling of goods at docks, quays or wharfs, but excluding transport by hand. Children under the age of 15 years shall not be employed or work...in occupation to which this Article applies which are scheduled as dangerous, or unhealthy by the competent authority."[6]

The Employment of Children Act, 1938 was passed to implement these conventions agreed upon by the International Labour Conference. Further, it raised the minimum age for handling goods in docks from 12 to 15 years. Furnishing certificate of age became mandatory. Employment of a child was thus regulated according to age group. In fact it is not as exhaustive as it is believed to be. It related itself particularly to (i) age of employment—below 15 employment was prohibited, and, (ii) procedure for certificate of age. A spate of amendments and new conventions followed from 1938 to 1940, 1941, 1944, 1945, 1946 and 1947. All these happened before we attained our Independence in August, 1947.

After Independence this humanitarian approach kept flowing without any abatement. The Constitution of India adopted on the 26th January, 1950 recognised the need for granting special protection to children both in the Fundamental Rights and the Directive Principles. These provisions are incorporated in Part III of the Constitution wherein Article 24 lays down "that no child below the age of 14 years shall be employed to work in any factory or mine or engaged in any other hazardous employment. State's action in this connection is beyond challenge.

Part IV of the Constitution mention the directive principles. Article 39 protects the children by explicitly mentioning that :

(a) Tender age of children are not abused and that citizens are not forced by economic necessity to enter avocations unsuited to their age and strength ;

(b) That children are given opportunities and facilities to develop in a healthy manner and in condition of

6. *Report on the Committee on Child Labour*, Government of India, 1981, p. 22.

freedom and dignity and that children and youth are protected against exploitation and against moral and material abandonment."

Article 45 directed the states for free education to all children within 10 years and Article 47 demanded nutrition and a good tiving standard for children. Gradually sense of constitutional philosophy comprising of ethical obligations towards social welfare developed in post 1950 periods in consequence of which numerous Acts were passed each bearing some affectionate and sympathetic attitude towards child labour. Thus the Act of 1933 and 1938 were followed by Minimum Wages Act of 1948. The Factories Act of 1948, the Plantation Labour Act, 1951, The Mines Act 1952, The Merchant Shipping Act, 1958, The Motor Transport Worker Act, 1961, The Atomic Energy Act, 1962, The Beedi and Cigar Worker (Conditions of Employment) Act, 1966, The Shops and Establishment Act in various states. They all prescribed sometimes the usual, some times specific age of children for occupation desirability, hours of works, rest, leisure, recreation etc.

The Children Act, 1960, as amended upto 1981 seeks to define children, hours of work, children's homes, the case of the neglected children, delinquent children, procedures in Courts to bring them to books, appeals and revision etc. Chapter VI of the said Act deals with special offences in respect of children and penalties connected with them, e.g., begging, intoxicating and other forms of cruelties.[7] The employment of children's Act, 1938 Para 3-D required each establishment to display the rules of employment and to maintain registers "in respect of children employed or permitted to work in pursuance of sub-section (2) of Section (3) in any occupation referred to in sub section (1) of that Section for inspection by an Inspector "at all

7. The Children Act, 1960 as ammended up to 1981, published by Delhi Law House.

times during working hours or when work is being carried on in such occupation, showing :

(a) the name and date of birth of every child under seventeen years of age so employed or permitted to work ;

(b) the periods of work of any such child and the intervals of rest to which he is entitled ;

(c) the nature of work of any such child, and

(d) such other particulars as may be presented."[8]

However, from actual observation it can be summarised that these Acts live more in denial than in acceptance, for hardly any silk weaving factory in Bhagalpur ever cares to display these instructions. Their implementations are a far-fetched dream—not yet, nor presently expected to materialise.

While the people's attitude towards legislative endeavours has been lukewarm and not properly co-operative, yet the nation has not been silent as regards the prevailing of child labour. The National Commission on Labour, 1969, reported that "Child labour persists in varying degrees in the unorganised sector such as small plantation, restaurants and hotels, cotton ginning and weaving, carpet weaving, stone breaking, brick-kiln, handicrafts and road building." This brought on the floor of the Parliament the Contract Labour Regulations and Abolition Act, 1970, but there is no specific protection for children who are seen building houses, and roads under contractors. Yet people's conscience was constantly hurt at the sight of labouring boys and girls, therefore, the Social Welfare Department under the Central Government established a working group in April, 1974, to study the various aspects of child labour in the country. Consequently, a National Children's Board was established in December, 1974 with the Prime

8. Labour Minor Acts, 1987, Ram Narain Lal Beni Prasad, Allahabad, p. 15.

Minister as the President. It has become an apex body with the Minister of Education and Social Welfare as working Chairman, and the Minister of Health and Family Planning, Members of Parliament, State's representatives as Executive Committee Members. The aims of the Board are laudable, as they attempt to draw public attentions towards the need of children, to review periodically the progress made in protecting the children, and to recommend to prevent such gaps etc.[9] November, 1975 saw another Seminar on "Employment of Children in India", organised by the National Institute of Public Corporation and Child Development. It advocated wide and pervasive education among children. It also resolved to evolve a National Children's Code with model rules, uniform standards governing employment of children in various sectors and vocations. The Seminar highlighted the necessity of social security to poor families who let out their children for labour. This is, indeed, a positive step forward to alleviate the troubles of economically unfortunate families. But the problems remain as vast and colossal in agriculture sector as they used to be even forty two years back, by which we mean the pre-Independence and early post-independent India. Possibly the same situation obtains everywhere in the developing countries, most particularly, in Africa.

One thing is certain that the child in India has not been overlooked in legislations. Right from the last part of the 19th century to the second decade in the 20th century, child welfare measures had begun and this period may be a time for initiation. The second period may be taken from 1921 to 1930 which is a time for great stirring in Indian history. Legislators call it a period of substantial progress towards protective legislation for children. The time-count from 1931-1949 takes us to a period of comparatively more concentrated effort to deal with child labour. It is a period of documentation and comprehensive Reports, as for example, by Royal Commissions.

9. Kulshreshtha, J.C. *Child Labour id India*, op. cit., pp. 57-58.

Finally we reach the span of time from 1950 to the present day which is indeed full of progressive activity and effective legislations protecting the Hostages of ill-luck, that is our children. The helping hands of academicians and voluntary organisations are distinctly visible in this period. It is a rich crop of valuable literature, legislation, suggestions and even useful attempts to save children from ignominy. But we have to see pragmatically how far we have succeeded in these pious and vigorous efforts, and if the goal is still far and distant, then we must discover what impedes our race to the destination.

Social awareness of these legislations is lacking among the respondents, that is the child and his/her parents. Only one mother had heard of some laws protecting the child which comes to about 0.40% out of a total of 250 respondents. Likewise 88.80 percent of fathers knew nothing about such legal enactments which would save their children from being exploited. When there is no awareness of legal measures, there can be no question of their implementation in social sphere. A gruesome picture arises on this account which we can see in Table Nos. 17, 18 and 19 of the Chapter on Interpretation of Data.

Concluding, therefore, the positive and negative aspects of governmental helpful legislations, we ought to realize that the efficiency of a weapon lies not in its possession, but in its application. We must develop mechanism to deliver the goods to the people who need it most. The village parents are ill-equipped to obtain information. As long as they wade in the mire of ignorance, there can be no hope of restoring them to a better health and dignified life. Slavery prospers where ignorance flourishes. Time has come when the honest labour of the government be taken to the remotest villages so that the rural children be no more put to the altar of exploitation.

CHAPTER VIII

Conclusion

Nature offers gold in sand and dust. It is for the goldsmith to turn it into a pleasant wedding ring.

Empirical research is like the goldsmith's job or the potter's who thumps his wet clay or the clod of saturated earth and presents beautiful cups and lovely idols. The present work is scientific, analytical, objective and perceptive with its hypothesis, sample and setting, all indicated in its title : "Child Labour in the Silk Industry of Bhagalpur : A Sociological Study".

Child labour is a burning problem of today and global also. The world is wide awake and considers it a socio-economic as well as, a psycho-social menace. Children living and working in an environment characterized by malnutrition, infection, poor housing, lack of safe water and sanitation and inadequate health care can have little chance of realizing their full economic, psychological, and social potential. Furthermore, "they will in turn give birth to another unhealthy generation, thus helping to perpetuate a vicious cycle".[1]

1. Mahler, Dr. N., Director General of World Health Organization, in *World Health Magazine*,, February-March, 1979. p, 1.

The Universal Declaration of Human Rights speaks in the following terms :

"Everyone has the right to a standard of living adequate for the health and well-being of himself and of his family, including food, clothing, housing, and medical care and necessary social services, and the right to security in the event of unemployment, sickness, disability, widowhood, old age or other lack of livelihood in circumstances beyond his control".

"Motherhood and Childhood are entitled to special care and assistance. All children, whether born in or out of wedlock, shall enjoy the same social protection."[2]

This Declaration and subsequent ones, say UNICEF's in 1959 and in 1979, the International Year of the Child, help us to recollect what the First Prime Minister of India, Pt. Jawahar Lal Nehru had said :

"Somehow the fact that ultimately everything depends on the human factor gets rather lost in our thinking of plans an d schemes of national development in terms of factories and machinery and general schemess....Ultimately, of course, it is the human being that counts, and if the human being counts, well, he counts much more as a child than as a grown-up".

Thus, quite validly, this research work spins round the working child, willy-nilly, the exploited child. Curiously enough, working children with sunken eyes and twisted bones are not seen in our ancient scriptures or historical texts. The Greek tradition mentions sales and pledging of children but not quite often. It is only with the advancement of human civilisation, the ushering in of steam engines and mills with chimneys or the progress of trade and monopolies that we come across slums and shanty dwellers, waifs, working as slaves or

2. Evang, Karl, Formerly Director General of Health Services, Norway, in *World Health Magazine*, Nov. 1973.

bonded labourers. Feudalism and Mercantilism sponsored child labour. Economic royalists cherish absolutism and with capitalism and colonialism taking long strides, liberty became a fallen angel and power over weak peoples became the most flagrant of all passions. Shelley rightly decried the avarice of his own countrymen and of other Europeans :

> "Power, like a desolating pestilence
> Pollutes, whate'er it touches, and obedience,
> Bane of all genius, virtue, freedom, truth,
> Makes slaves of men, and of the human frame
> A mechanical automation".[3]

Thus behind the story of the five to fourteen years kids melting their energies in workhouses, lies the element of avarice and possessiveness over plenty, ripening in the hearts of a few soulless people.

Silk manufacture and silk-trade are ancient business of India and China and recent ones of Italy, America, Spain and other countries in the West. Since silk manufacture is a delicate work, the deft hands of tender children help to perform the initial jobs of the trade. Child labour is, therefore, favoured in silk manufacture, just as it is favoured in carpet weaving, matches industry or filigree work. History records that a full-scale trade in silk developed during the East India Company rule in India, and Bhagalpur silk had its due share of importance in silk export to European Countries in the Dutch, French and English Ships. Bhagalpur excelled in Eri, Tassar, Monga and Mulberry silk along with Baftah which was also produced Rajmahal and Maldah districts.

While tt is reported that silk manufacture is on the decline in U.S.A. with the advent of nylon and other synthetic fabrics, India maintains its level of production and export, thus helping to cut down its adverse balance in international trade. Behind

3. Shelley, Percy Bysrshe—Queen Mab.

such a significant and magnificant effort, we should not miss the contribution of the child worker of Bhagalpur.

Before we proceed into details it seems just and proper to discuss the first term of the topic—'Child labour'. What makes child labour detestable, when all 'child labour' cannot be condemned. A child in an Ashram of ancient sages doing lessons in agriculture, tending cattle, and offering manual services (कृषि, गोरक्षा, परिचर्या) was a part of value-based education scheme where kings and nobles sent their sons and daughters for training. Likewise, the National Basic Education System where every student was required to do manual work, and undergo crafts training surely deserved approbation and not condemnation. Any occupation for the child which has a purpose, plan and freedom and is not oppressive to him is a useful training. Whereas when his energies are spent in seeking his own survival or his family's and the development of his latent faculties as a human being is retarded, the process becomes a social evil and the product becomes a vicious annihilation of the child. Wage-earning by a child comes into direct conflict with his unfettered growth and natural development. It is here then that child labour falls into disrepute. Such a phenomenon in the silk industry of Bhagalpur is the real object of our study where we may painfully discover the element of exploitation by the employers. Finally, the picture that emerges before us is of a boa-constrictor, a big reptile wrapping itself round the body of an unclaimed infant lying alone in a part of Jungle.

Obviously then, we have to ponder—what promotes child labour in our society ? Is it simply a socio-economic or psycho-social problem ? Does child labour spring from growing industrialisation where disparity in economic level is too great ? Does it arise from poverty in rural areas and assume menacing proportions in urban areas ? Is it a resultant factor of urbanization, migration from villages to cities, and a bit of craze for modernization ? Is it because of explosion of population in developing countries where resources for subsistence are not in plenty ? Is it because child labour is cheaper as compared to adult labour, or does child labour prosper with the dignified aim of acquiring skill in any trade which may help in future life ?

All these have been discussed in Chapter two and subsequent ones where, of course, exploitation of the child is the central theme and the denial of a child's rights over the society is the single anxiety.

Nearly 10.7 million children are at work in India. The maximum number of work-bound children are in Andhra Pradesh, and the minimum in Kerala. In between them are Maharashtra, Tamil Nadu, West Bengal, Bihar, Gujarat, Rajasthan and Uttar Pradesh. It is also worth noticing that these figures do not include rural children whose labours are not wage oriented and who participate freely in unorganised sector of family agriculture endeavours. Urban child labour is wage oriented since most of them are run away boys who work in sales departments, or domestic cooks, errand boys in companies, house keepers, waiters, shop assistants, coolies and the like.

Child labour in silk industry of Bhagalpur is mainly employed in fourteen initial jobs which are preparatory before the yarns are put on the looms. Even waste threads are collected and are utilised as laces for amulets and other ornaments which is prepared into different shining patterns by boys and girls assisting silk manufacture.

Such vast efforts in cottage industries like the silk manufacture at Bhagalpur and elsewhere should have amply drawn the attention of surveyors, report compilers, statisticians, social workers and jurists also. But it may be regretted that this has escaped their attention leading to the perpetuation of the evil practice of child labour in Bhagalpur.

Naturally, therefore, there is scarcity of published materials on the issue of child labour in India until the call came from

UNICEF under the aegis of UNO. England and America had produced literature of great merit on the distressed children of the soil, but India had made no such efforts, nor the developing countries too. World War I left million children as destitutes, but by the time the world could take notice of them World War II started and its devastation was unspeakable. But the founding of United Nations Organization came as a boon, and its agencies WHO., FAO, UNICEF, UNESCO, ILO and others made stupendous efforts to draw world-wide attention towards the fate of children who were slowly crippling and were joining the caravan of death. Literature on children, novels, short stories, sketches, poems, dramas and journalistic reports appeared in plenty touching the conscience of the people round the globe. Even legislators, jurists and medical personnel came forward with their suggestions which were remarkably utilitarian and greatly protective. Bihar too contributed its share and submitted reports about the plight of the working children. Voluntary organizations joined hands in vitalising such an awakening : the flood-gates were opened, and children came under full focus. Investigative reports about working children in Delhi, Calcutta, Patna, Madras, Bombay, Ahmedabad and other places came one after another which were taken notice of by eminent journals and newspapers. Courts were asked to treat severely cases of harassment and torture of labouring children according to laws enacted for their safety. The Centre asked the states to enact legal measures in favour of children. UNICEF declared 1979 as International Year of the Child (IYC) and repeated the Declaration of the Rights of the Children which were unanimously adopted by all the countries : developing and the developed alike. A revolution mitigating child's difficulties was gloriously complete—what remained was the consolidation of the fruits of revolution by each country in its own way.

Here the necessity of proving the taste of the pudding arose, and a better scheme than utilising an Interview Schedule was difficult to find. A rigorous and vigorous, scientific and logical, objective and impersonal method of investigation, which is another name for empirical research, was adopted to reach people's perspectives, and inner reactions. As such a well representing population stratum comprising of 250 men and women was contacted, mainly working children, who comprised our respondents. They were our sample who were inhabitants of Bhagalpur Municipal Corporation's different wards and zones which was in fact our setting of geographical background. Sample and setting comprised our universe. The respondents were broken up under three variables, viz, socio-economic profiles, age-group, and income strate. Data came profusely on person to person contact or interviews which are divided into two parts :

(1) personal identification of the respondent, and

(2) occupational relationship, i.e. between employer-employee, respondent and his job, which reflected their pleasures and pains.

The task was fulfilled chearfully and it brought out a great amount of informations about child labour in the silk industry of Bhagalpur, that were hitherto unknown.

While child labour is rampant in the developing countries, India being a leading country in this regard is yet obsessed with child labour. Particularly in the silk industry of Bhagalpur, children have to perform varieties of jobs, some of which create physical deformity, chemical disasters and in the final analysis dull their sensibility. This is only a natural hazard for children of 5 to 7 years of age working sitting or standing for long hours. Absence of proper sanitation, lack of safe drinking water and arrangement for ablutions, inadequate light and clean air quite often induce serious sickness. About 86.40% complained of such disadvantages in their workhouses. Only 13.60% were fortunate to work in healthy surroundings. It is true that Labour Acts make leisure hours imperative, but they are few and far between. 45.41% respondents informed that they had a daily leisure of 30 minutes ; 12.97% had 60 mts leisure, whereas 41.62% said they enjoyed 45 mts of leisure. Sundays for Hindus and Fridays for Muslim child labour were weekly off days, there was nothing like a casual leave or earned leave privilege in silk manufacturing houses.

Labour and wages are never commensurate with each other where there is a grain of exploitation involved. It is inconceivable in present day's price-rise that 37.20% children will be satisfied with an earning of Rs. 5,- a day and 49.20% of them happy with Rs. 6/- to Rs. 10/- per day. Even 13.60% children getting Rs. 15/- per day (monthly 25 days only) that is Rs. 375/- a month would be considered to add to his family income adequately. The amount cannot today meet the cost of essential commodities for one person, leave alone 5 to 6 persons. But compulsions have their own philosophy : they compel men to believe in destiny, an unkind God, and cruel times. While 77.59% of respondents (earning Rs. 5000/- annually) were disgruntled at what they received as wages, 20.69% earning upto Rs. 10,000/- annually were reconciled with their lots and those lucky enough to soar above that amount thanked their Lord, and God, and their fate, although they comprised only 1.72%. Little did they realise that their monthly income came upto Rs. 1250/-, still inadequate for a big family of six persons. Wage disparity between a labourer earning Rs. 450/- a month on an average, and an official getting Rs. 7000/- a month is an invitation to rebellion on road, a common sight that we see in the form of scuffles in the fish market or vegetable mandi between salesman and the purchasers or between a rickshaw puller and his passenger.

Naturally, job satisfaction is sheer wishful thinking. On enquiry, 74.80% respondents expressed dis-satisfaction, only 23.60% took it easy and 1.60% had nothing to say. Since insecurity looms large before the respondents, and an eternal stalemate, since there is no avenue of promotion or increments in these jobs, one has to take things passively, even slavishly.

Most of them are casual labour (61.20%) while 38% are temporary, as such, no voice of protest can be raised, no demand notice can be served for one reason exclusively that children do not have a trade union.

Earning, whether big or small, brings self-confidence (52.40%), but economic independence can come only when earning matches daily demands. 82.80% respondents expressed that economic independence is a day-dream with the wages earned by them.

Illiteracy and poverty make men hollow. When compounded they turn children vagrant, immoral, wasteful and reckless. Smoking Biris, running to Cinema halls, snatching a few drinks on occasions are the easy alluring vices. The influence of urbanity only adds to their deadliness. Greed for costly things, a wrist watch, a transistor, good clothes, and a bicycle captivates them, and frustration takes them to the dark lanes of criminality.

To retrieve children from way-wardness people look to the laws if they can help. From the first half of this passing century laws have been promulgated to save children from exploitation and misuse. But when 88.80% of parents confess their ignorance of such beneficial laws, then woe betide them: to save their children is difficult. An ignorant mass lives taking everything as providence's decree. Yet those who are at the helm of affairs should bring awareness of legal measures at the doors of the unenlightened people whether they live in villages or in cities. Until this is done, the children of Bhagalpur engaged in silk industry will continue to suffer.

We need, therefore, to point out in brief what these laws are and how can they be placed before the people whom these laws serve. With the passing of the Apprentices Act in 1850, Guardianship and Wards Act of 1890, and Factories Act of 1881, care and concern for children has been witnessed. Eight different Acts have been passed between 1881 and 1961 which go to define children, hours of work, leisure, sanitation and suitable labour for them. But the drastic change in our outlook towards children came after World War II. If the United Nations Organization brought about a total transformation in political vision, its off shoots, the UNICEF ushered a complete mutation in the social milieu affecting the child. Its wisdom, perception and motivation have been upheld by World communities represented by SAARC and such other Organizations, like the International Labour organization, the National Children Board of India and others. The Indian Constitution has upheld the rights of children to save living both in the Fundamental Rights and the Directive Principles. Consequently, the Employment of Children Act, 1939 have defined children to mean boys and girls within 15 years, their hours of work up to 6 hours, and restrictions over their employment in dangerous jobs. This was further amended by the Children Act of 1960, amended upto 1981, where the employers called upon to display rules of employment on notice boards in their work houses, and these would be liable for inspection by Government officers.

But Bhagalpur silk industry in general do not seem to honour these rules. There is an atmosphere of *status quo*: things stand today where they were fifty years back. This is because social awareness about these legal measures is absent (Table 17, 18, 19 may please be seen) and if such conditions are allowed to continue, then improvement in children's plight will remain a far cry. We should remember the great political thinker, Dr. Ram Manohar Lohia, in this connection. He had once solemnly observed : "The abstract which is not translated into concrete, and speech which is not followed by action only exposes the emptiness and irrelevance of all political, and social activity."[4] Exploitation of the working child is a special class of apartheid which must be fought to the finish. The fight shall

4. Quoted by George Fernandes in the *Illustrated Weekly*, January 29 to February 4, 1989, p. 30.

have two fronts : one, the socio-economic frame of the working child must change by improving their financial conditions, and secondly, the employer must be humanized so that he does not indulge in ruthless exploitation of these blossoms of the dust. All fatalistic approach must be removed from the child mind ; this will be our fight against his psycho-social make up. The obnoxious practices of the employer must also go, as any criminality must go, so that the child breathes freely, enjoys his work and becomes proud of his country. This process cannot brook any delay. The child must be assured of a bright Tomorrow by offering him a Joyous Today. This is what is immediately needed and is in keeping with Declarations issued during the International Year of the Child (IYOC-1979). If the UNICEF has suggested an International summit over this issue—care and concern for the child—the suggestion is most welcome.

Bibliography

Ackoff, R.L., The Design of Social Research, Univ. of Chicago, 1953.

Agnihotri, W., Techniques of Social Research, M.N. Publishers, New Delhi, 1930.

Agrawal, Lakshman Das, Labour Minor Acts, Law Publishers, Allahabad, 1987.

Agrawala, A.N., Indian Labour Problems (Ed). Allahabad, 1947.

Aikin, Olga & Reid Judith, Labour Law Employment Welfare and Safety at Work, Penguin Book Ltd, U.K. 1971.

Albion, G.T., Labour Problems and Labour Law, Prentice Hall Inc., New York, 1963.

Alexander, N.C. Soviet Labour Law, University Book House, Delhi, 1961.

Alikhan, N & Ayesha, N., Status of Rural Women in India, Uppal Publishing House, New Delhi, 1981.

Altekar, A.S., The Position of Women in Hindu Civilization, Motilal Banarsidas, Benaras, 1956.

Aphale, C.A., Growing Up in an Urban Complex, National, New Delhi, 1976.

August, Aichhora, Wayward Youth, Imago Publishing Co. Ltd., London, 1950.

Baig, Tara Ali, Our Children, Govt. of India, New Delhi, 1979.

Balkanji Bari, Home & the World, 6, Gulistan, Bombay.

Beveridge, A.J., Child Labour in the Meaning of the Times & Other Speeches—Indianapolis, U.S.A., 1908.

Beveridge, W.I.B., The Art of Scientific Investigation, Norton, 1950.

Buchanan, Francis, Journals kept during the Survey of the District of Bhagalpur in 1810-1811 Govt. Press, Patna, 1930.

The Bible.

Carstairs, G.M., Twice Born, Mogarth Press, London, 1957.

Chandrashekhar, S., Infant Mortality, Population Growth, and Family Planning, Allen & Unwin, London, 1972.

Chatterjee, B.B., Impact of Social Legislation on Social Change, The Minerva Associate, Calcutta, 1971.

Clifford, Manshardt, The Child in India, Bombay, 1953.

Cohen, M.R. & E. Nagel, An Introduction to Logic and Scientific Method, Harcount, 1934.

Cochran, W.G., Sampling Techniques—Wiley, 1953.

Coiletta, N.J. and N. Donohue, The Ecology of Child Development in a Malayasian Rubber Plantation, I.C.W.R., 1977.

Costin, Lela B., Child Welfare, Policies & Practice, Mcgraw Hill Book Company, 1979.

David, M. and Irene Lezine, Early Child Care in France, Gordon & Breach, London, 1975.

de Souza, Alfred, Children in Creches: Day Care for the Urban under privileged, Intellectual Publishing House, New Delhi, 1979.

—do—Children in India, Critical Issues in Human Development, Manohar, New Delhi, 1979.

Dubey, S.M., Social Mobility Among the Professions, Bombay, 1972.

Dutta, R.C., Early Hindu Civilization, Punthi Pustak, Calcutta, 1963.

Encyclopaedia Americana, U.S.A. 1981.

Encyclopedia of Social Sciences.

Felt, Jeremy P. Hostages of Fortune : Child Labour Reforms in New York State, Syracuse University Press, 1965.

Fuller, H., The International Handbook of Child Care and Protection, Longmen's Green & Co. London, 1928.

Fuller, R.G., Child Labour and the Constitution. The Thomas Y. Crowell Co., New York 1923.

Gandhi, M.K., India of my Dreams. Hind Kitab Ltd., Bombay, 1947.

George, K.N., Child Labour in the City of Madras, 1975 (A paper).

Gettel, R.G., Modern Political Theory, World Press, Calcutta, 1950.

Giri, V.V., Labour Problem in Industry, Asia Publishing House, Bombay, 1958.

Godde, W.J. & Hatt, P.K. Methods in Social Research, Mc-graw Hill, Tokyo, 1952.

Gohen, Frank, J., Children in Trouble, W.N. Norton Co., New York, 1952.

Gokhale, S.D. and Neera K. Sohani, Child in India, Somaiya, Bombay, 1979.

Gopalan, C. et al, Diet Atlas of India, National Institute of Nutrition, Hyderabad, 1971.

Gore, M.S., Urbanization and Family Change, Popular Prakashan, Bombay, 1968.

Gazetteer of Bhagalpur, Edited, Govt. of Bihar, Patna.

Horowitz, E.L. and R.B. Horrowitz, Development of Social Attitudes in Children, 1938.

Hurlock, B. Elizabeth, Adolescent Development, Mcgraw Hill Books Co. Inc. New York.

Hyman, H.H., Survey, Design and Analysis : Principles, Cases & Procedures—Free Press, 1955.

Jahoda, Marie, Research Methods in Social Relations U.S.A., 1962.

Jahoda, M. & S.W. Cook, Security Measures and Freedom of Thought, Yale Law Journal, 61, 1952.

Jain, S.N. and Usha Loghani, Child and Law, New Delhi, 1979.

Jennings, H.H., Leadership & Isolation, Longmans, 1950.

Kaur, Surjit, Wastage of Children, Sterling Publishers, New Delhi, 1978.

Khalakdina, Margaret, Early Child Care in India, Gordan & Breach, London, 1979.

Kothari, C.R., Research Methodology, Wiley Eastern Ltd, 1985.

Kulshreshtha, J.C., Child Labour in India, New Delhi, 1978.

Legouis & Cazamian, A History of English Literature, London, 1951.

Leighton, A.H., Human Relations in a Changing World, Dutton, 1949.

Lumpkin, K.D. and Doughlas, D.W., Child Workers in America, Robert M.M.C. Bride & Co., New York, 1937.

Lundberg, G.A., Social Research, Longman's Green & Co., New York, 1942.

Maccoby, E.E. and N. Maccoby, The Interview—A Tool of Social Science, Addison, Wesley, 1954.

Mangold, George B., Problems of Child Welfare, Macmillan Co., New York.

Martin, Montgomery, Eastern India, Vol. I-III, Delhi, 1976.

McCarthy, P.J., Sample Design in Research Methods in Social Relations, Dryden, 1951.

McChelland, D.C., Personality, Dryden, 1951.

Mc Iver, R.M., The Elements of Social Science, Mathuen & Co, London, 1956.

Merton, R.K., Social Theory & Social Structure, Free Press, 1957.

Merton, R.K. & M. Fiske. A Curtis, Mass Persuasion Harper, 1946.

Muckerjee, R., The Indian Working Class, Hind Kitab, Bombay, 1951.

Mukherjee, D.P., Problems of Indian Youth, Hind Kitabs, Bombay, 1946.

Pant, I.P., Child Welfare in India, Ministry of Education, Delhi, 1963.

Paul Choudhury, D., Child Welfare & Development, Atmaram & Sons, Delhi, 1980.

—do—Child Welfare Manual, Atmaram & Sons, Delhi, 1980.

Payre, S.L., The Art of Asking Questions—Princeton University, 1951.

Picholiya, K.R., Child Labour in a Metropolitan City—A Study of Ahmedabad, 1980.

Rowntree, B.S., Poverty & Progress, Longmans 1941.

Saran, K.M., Labour in Ancient India, Vora & Co., Publication Pvt. Ltd., Bombay, 1957.

Sen, Padmini, Child Labour as a Social Problem (Article Contributed in Child Labour in India).

Shakespeare, W., Works, Henry IV, O.U.P.

Shamasastri, R., Kautilaya's Arthashastra, Vol. III, Mysore, 1967.

Singh, Musafir & Nath, Nagendra, Children in Delhi Slum—A Survey of Their Life Condition, New Delhi, 1974.

Singh, Musafir & V.D. Kaur & S.A. Khan, Working Children in Bombay—A Study, New Delhi, National Institute of Public Cooperation & Child Development, 1978.

Smart, Mollie S., Children Development and Relationships, U.S.A., 1967.

Tilak, V.R.K., A Survey of Labour in India Atmaram & Sons, Delhi, 1950.

Venkatsubhaiyay, M., Indian Economy Since Independence, Asia Publishing House, Bombay, 1961.

Wilkinson & Bhandarkar, Methodology & Techniques of Social Research, Himalayan Pub. : House, Bombay, 1977.

William, F.H., Our Children, Oriental Watchman Publication House, Pune, 1951.

Wilson, C.R., The Early Annals of English in Bengal, Vol. I-III, New Delhi, 1983.

Wood, S.D., Constitutional Politics in the Progressive Era—Child Labour and the Laws, the University of Chicago, 1968.

Wordsworth, William, Works.

Zeitz, Dorothy, Child Welfare—Principles and Methods, John Wiley & Sons, Inc., New York, 1959.

Books in Hindi and Sanskrit

1. Goswami Tulsidas, Ram Charitamanasa
2. Rigveda
3. Manusmriti
4. Kautilya's Arthashastra
5. Satpatha Brahmana
6. Saraswati, Dayanand Maharshi, Satyartha Prakasha
7. —do— Rigveda Bhasya Bhumika
8. Sharma, Vishnu—Hitopadesa

9. Taittariyopanisad

10. Valmiki Ramayana

Reports

1. Seminar Reports :

   (1) New Frontiers in Child Welfare ICCW—1952 and 1956

   (2) A National Policy for Children—ICCW—1964

   (3) Pre-School Child—ICCW 1970

2. UNICEF Reports—

   (1) Children of Developing Countries— 1963

   (2) Children understress— 1970

   (3) Statistical Profile of Children Youth in India 1977

3. World Health Organization Magazine—Reports.

4. India International Centre, Quarterly, 4, N.I. 1977 (T. Ali Baig)

5. Social Scientist—Political Issues in Health, Population, and Nutrition, 73-74, Aug-Sept 1978 (Article by D. Banerjee).

6. Assignment Children—Swaminathan Mina's Article—The Pre-School Child, Jan-March 1973

7. Reports of Tata Institute of Social Sciences—Bombay.

   (1) The Handicapped Child—by Wadia, A.R.

   (2) Child in the Urban Community—A Survey of Problem Area of Bombay City, 1975 by Mehta, B.H. & A.R. Pardiwala.

8. Report of the Juvenile Delinquency in India, Children Aid Society, Bombay, 1956.

9. Research and Evolution of Child Welfare, International Union for Child Welfare Congress, Hague, 1966.

10. Report of Parliamentary Committee—A Programme for Child Welfare, 1969.

11. Indian Council for Child Welfare (ICCW)—Indian Concept for Child Welfare : Working Children in Urban Delhi, New Delhi, 1977.

12. Promoting Healthy Child—Growth and Value of Children Concept—A Framework—NIPHC—Document No. 16 Working Children in Urban Delhi, Govt. of India, 1977.

13. Report on the Working and Living Condition of Workers in the Building Construction Industry in Delhi, Ministry of Labour, Labour Bureau, Chandigarh, 1978.

14. National Institute of Labour Corporation and Child, Development, New Delhi, 1978.

15. Annual Report of the Year 1978-79, Central Social Welfare Board, New Delhi.

16. World Atlas of the Child, Washington D.C., World Bank, 1979.

17. Report on the Committee on Child Labour, Nasik, Govt. of India Press, 1981.

18. The State of the World Children, N.Y. (U.S.A.) UNICEF, 1989.

19. Child Labour in Kerala's Coir Industry—Study of a Few Selected Village—Centre for Development Studies, 1980.

20. Exploitation of Children in Informal Sector—Some Proposition for Research, I.L.O. Geneva, 1980.

21. Bihar Labour Deptt. (Factory)—Annual Report on the Working of the Employment of Children Act, 1938 for the year 1963, Ranchi.

22. Child Labour in Patna—Anugrah Narayan Sinha Institute of Social Sciences, 1979.

23. Match Industry in Sivakasi—Madras Institute of Development Studies, 1985.

24. Census of India, 1981.

25. Sociological Abstracts 1981-86.
26. The Children's Act, 1960 amended upto 1981.
27. Labour Minor Acts.
28. Why Child Labour Laws—U.S.A., Deptt. of Labour, Children's Bureau, 1906.

Newspapers and Magazines

1. The Statesman.
2. The Times of India, Delhi & Patna.
3. The Hindusthan Times, Delhi, Patna.
4. Dharmayuga.
5. Manohar Kahaniya
6. Social Welfare
7. The Illustrated Weekly of India
8. All India Radio News Bulletin.
9. Television National Network—News (Samachar)

Index